THE STORY OF THE 2023 MICHIGAN
WOLVERINES' LEGENDARY RUN TO
THE NATIONAL CHAMPIONSHIP

Blue Reign!

Detroit Free Press

THE LINEUP

EDITOR

Gene Myers

DESIGNER

Ryan Ford

COPY CHIEF

Owen Davis

COPY EDITOR

Jennifer Troyer

HEADLINES

Ryan Ford

GAME RECAPS

Gene Myers,
Free Press staff

PROJECT COORDINATOR

Kirkland Crawford

COVER DESIGNER

Ryan Ford

PHOTO IMAGING

Ryan Ford

FREE PRESS WRITERS

Tony Garcia, Rainer Sabin, Jared Ramsey, Shawn Windsor, Jeff Seidel, Mitch Albom, Chris Solari, Ryan Ford, Kirkland Crawford, Gene Myers

FREE PRESS PHOTOGRAPHERS

Kirthmon F. Dozier, Junfu Han, Melanie Maxwell

SPECIAL THANKS

Nicole Avery Nichols, Noah Amstadter, Lisa Hein, Josh Williams, Megan Holt, Michael Kern, Eros, Schrodinger & Bobo.

IN MEMORIAM
KIRTHMON F. DOZIER: 1958-2024

DANIEL MEARS/USA TODAY SPORTS

Kirthmon F. Dozier Sr. was supposed to shoot pictures of the Rose Bowl on New Year's Day for the *Detroit Free Press*. Instead, he watched it from a hospital bed with his children — a rare time for all of them to enjoy a major sporting event together.

"I was always the one dropping him off at the airport," son Kirt Dozier Jr. said. "It was kind of cool to watch Michigan win with him."

Overtime was a bonus; recognizing the importance of the situation, the hospital staffers who'd been chasing them away all week at 8 p.m. looked the other way.

"He was glued to it," Kirt Jr. said, and it turned out to be his final game.

Dozier Sr., 65, who covered thousands of professional, college and high school events and even multiple Olympics for the *Free Press* across 28 years, died Jan. 5, 2024, after a brief illness. He attended Washington State and then worked for the *Bellingham (Wash.) Herald*, the *Detroit News* and *Newsday* of Long Island, New York. He returned to Detroit with the *Free Press* in 1995.

While he also handled news assignments, he was best known for his work in sports and was an expected part of the game-day scene for teams and fans.

J. Kyle Keener, a former *Free Press* chief photographer, described Dozier in more frenzied prose than his low-key friend ever used: "Just the kind of guy that you wanted in that photographic hot seat when the pressure cooker was turned up high and it was time to produce tremendous quality imagery under extreme deadline conditions."

– NEAL RUBIN

Detroit Free Press

TRIUMPH BOOKS

TRIUMPHBOOKS.COM
@TriumphBooks

ISBN: 978-1-63727-662-4

▶▶▶ Triumph Books LLC
▶▶▶ Phone: (312) 337-0747

▶▶▶ 814 North Franklin Street, Chicago, Illinois 60610

BLUE REIGN!

1 THE VICTORS

4

What happens when the nation's top defense meets the nation's top passing game? Domination, as the Wolverines shut down the Heisman runner-up, then romped to their first title since 1997.

2 THE SEASONS

18

After so many repeats, it was a season of firsts: The first program to 1,000 wins. The first Black head coach during a game. The first coach to win back-to-back-to-back outright Big Ten titles.

3 THE CHAMPS

100

Once again, the season came down to this: Three games for a championship — the Big Ten title game in Indianapolis, the Rose Bowl in Pasadena, and then, finally, the CFP title game in Houston.

1

THE VICTORS

After a season of trying to ignite the ground game, the Wolverines caught fire just in time to torch their foe in the CFP title game — and finally bring national championship No. 12 home to the Big House.

In his ninth season at Michigan, Jim Harbaugh reached the highest of mountaintops: U-M became the fourth champs to go 15-0, following Clemson (2018), LSU (2019) and Georgia (2022).
JUNFU HAN/DETROIT FREE PRESS

HAIL STORM

En route to raising the championship trophy, quarterback J.J. McCarthy raised his record as a starter to 27-1. In the championship game, McCarthy's most important play wasn't a pass but a scramble for 22 yards, Michigan's only third-down conversion.

After so long out in the championship cold, the Wolverines rode a maelstrom of clutch plays all the way to CFP glory.

By Mitch Albom

And then, all Hail broke loose.

Mike Sainristil intercepted a fourth-down pass, a desperate heave by Washington's Michael Penix Jr. that landed right in Sainristil's gut. He took off the other way, eyes widening. Ten yards. Twenty yards. Thirty yards. As tens of thousands of maize-and-blue fans who stuffed the stands of Houston's NRG Stadium rose and roared and waved the kid on.

Yes, he wore sunglasses at night. Mike Sainristil donned the Turnover Buffs and posed with the CFP championship trophy.

When Michael Penix Jr.'s pass sailed over wide receiver Jalen McMillan, nickelback Mike Sainristil plucked it from the sky and returned it 81 yards. It was his team-high sixth interception of the season.

He crossed midfield, green turf ahead. Fifty yards. Sixty yards. ...

And as Sainristil galloped on, all the shadows seemed to fall away, everything that hovered over this crazy, undefeated Wolverines season, the critics, the finger pointing, the suspensions, the Michigan vs. Everybody T-shirts, all of it, burned off as if hurtling into the sun.

Michigan would capture a national championship, its first in 26 years. No polls this time. No tying with another school. This was undeniable. A No. 1 ranking. A perfect season.

"What were you thinking as you were running that interception back?" Sainristil was asked on the stadium field, long after Michigan defeated Washington, 34-13, for the national crown.

He shook his head and laughed. "I couldn't breathe from when I caught that interception until about 10 minutes ago."

Well. That would be a superhuman act. Then again, this sort of felt like one, didn't it? Taking the final flag in this long, grueling race that started on a warm Labor Day weekend in Ann Arbor and ended a week after New Year's on a rainy Monday in a

Entering the championship game, junior tailback Donovan Edwards had rushed for 393 yards and three touchdowns. His longest run had been 22 yards. Against Washington, he scored on 41- and 46-yard runs and finished with 104 yards for his six carries.

massive Houston stadium?

It took an offense that plowed for more than 300 yards rushing for the night. It took a defense that threw a net over the explosive Penix, whose release was as fast as a lizard's tongue.

It took a numerically dominant performance that by itself still wouldn't have gotten it done — if not for key moments of executed opportunity.

Like Donovan Edwards breaking free for two massive touchdown runs.

Like cornerback Will Johnson whacking, juggling and finally snagging a Penix pass for a critical interception.

Like quarterback J.J. McCarthy, deep in his territory with the game tilting the wrong way, taking a third-down snap and breaking through the line, running past defend-

After his big night, Donovan Edwards owned the second- and third-longest touchdown runs in CFP history.

ers for 22 yards, his longest scramble of the season — and Michigan's only third-down conversion of the night.

One third-down conversion? And they won by three touchdowns?

Hey. Timing is everything.

"A glorious win," coach Jim Harbaugh said. "I could not be prouder or happier of our team. Fifteen-and-oh. Took on all comers. Last one standing."

All Hail breaks loose.

NOW OR NEVER

"Yeah, baby!" came the guttural cries. "Yeah, we did it!" Player after player smashed shoulder pads, lifted one another off the turf or filmed themselves shrieking in confetti-covered giddiness as family and friends surrounded them on the playing field.

It's in moments like these that you were reminded that college football was still a young man's game, in some ways a kid's game. Money, NIL or transfer portals couldn't change that.

Here was a group of believers who had to play almost half the season without their coach. Many of them came back after two previous losses in the College Football Playoff to get one more shot at the brass ring.

"The urgency," McCarthy said, in explaining what made this team click. "Right after that last game last year" — a 51-45 playoff loss to TCU — "it was different. I knew it. Just from being on the podium last year and saying we would be back. ... I had this feeling that it was going to be where we are right now."

Well. He might not have

When J.J. McCarthy threaded the needle with a fourth-quarter pass over the middle, Colston Loveland corralled it and ran for a 41-yard gain.
JUNFU HAN/ DETROIT FREE PRESS

seen the exact layout of the championship game, which wiggled like an earthworm from one team to the other.

Here, for posterity, was a recap of how the trophy was won.

A PATH TO GLORY

Remember that big college football games often could feel like Russian novels. This night was no exception. It had more momentum changes than a demolition derby. Michigan stole the early scenes, scoring on its first drive without seeing a third down, when Edwards broke from a scrum and raced outside, 41 yards, all the way to pay dirt.

Just like that, it was 7-0.

Then, on their next drive, the Wolverines hit the repeat button. This time, Edwards broke free for a 46-yard score, using great vision to burst to an open gap and race to glory. Edwards, the junior who had disappeared for much of the

MELANIE MAXWELL/DETROIT FREE PRESS

Ring it up! Quarterback J.J. McCarthy and tailback Blake Corum pointed to the finger that would don championship jewelry. Corum ensured a ring-sizing event with two fourth-quarter touchdowns.

season, had come back like a Marvel sequel. For a while, it looked as if he would be the story of the night.

But as we said, college football changed moods like a hungry freshman at a vending machine. After the Michigan defense squeezed as much

juice as possible out of Penix and his high-flying passing machine — holding Washington to just three points and some missed opportunities — Harbaugh let his confidence get the best of him.

With just under five minutes left in the first half, U-M

faced a fourth-and-two at the Washington 38. The team went to snap the ball for a punt. But Harbaugh called a sudden timeout. He motioned his players over. For some reason, he decided to go for the yards instead.

Bad idea. McCarthy, under pressure, threw a pass meant for Roman Wilson that was broken up, and instead of pinning the Huskies deep in their own territory and continuing the slow demoralization of their offense, Michigan gave them life.

And they took it. Washington marched downfield behind Penix and hung a fourth-down touchdown on the board with less than a minute remaining in the half to make it 17-10.

Suddenly, with the Washington players celebrating and their fans roaring to life, a game that felt lopsided most of the first half felt suddenly almost ... even.

And even it would stay

Offensive coordinator Sherrone Moore, a former offensive lineman, celebrated Michigan's national championship by lifting a former quarterback, Jim Harbaugh.
MELANIE MAXWELL/DETROIT FREE PRESS

MELANIE MAXWELL/ DETROIT FREE PRESS

When Mike Sainristil picked off a pass in the fourth quarter, his teammates jumped at the opportunity to block for him.

for much of the second half. What was billed as two high-flying offenses became all about defense. Stop and stop again. The two teams traded field goals in the third quarter, they traded six straight punts. The game was slogging. But the threat of Penix and a big pass play loomed large, something that could strike at any moment, like waiting for lightning in a thunderstorm. You knew it was coming. You just didn't know when.

Until finally, with just under 10 minutes left in the game, Michigan stopped waiting for the lightning and made some thunder of its own. McCarthy spotted tight end Colston Loveland over the middle and threw high. But Loveland leapt for it, snagged the ball and bolted for 41 yards.

It seemed to shake Michigan out of a fog.

A few plays later, Blake Corum wriggled off defenders and zipped up the middle for a touchdown and a 14-point cushion. The team mobbed him.

The Huskies, like a bull in the arena sensing defeat,

were wobbly on their hooves. All that remained was one last stop. It came on that fourth-down pass, with 4:46 left and Washington threatening on the Michigan 30-yard line.

Penix felt pressure. He threw badly. The ball went to Sainristil. And the young man who was born in Port-au-Prince, Haiti, and fled with his family as an infant was suddenly all the way at the end of opportunity's rainbow, a pot of championship gold waiting.

He made it 81 yards before being brought down. A few plays later, Corum punched it in for the final touchdown of the season and a certain victory.

"It means everything," Sainristil gushed while standing on the field and gazing at the cheering crowd. "All my life, God has blessed me and my family. ... All the kids back home in Haiti: Believe!"

Note: He was breathing when he said this.

CHECKING BOXES

The victory puts a snowy cap on the mountainous

season of Michigan football. When you start with your coach suspended against East Carolina and finish with him suspended against Ohio State, well, you know it's not a normal year.

In between you had a string

of undefeated performances, including a 49-0 drubbing of Michigan State, 32 straight running plays to defeat Penn State, and a 26-0 shutout to win the Big Ten championship. You had Sherrone Moore dropping F-bombs in effusing

JUNFU HAN/DETROIT FREE PRESS

Coach Jim Harbaugh checked in with cornerback Will Johnson, selected the defensive player of the game.

Spartans? That's history. Can't win the Big Ten? Done it multiple times. Can't win a playoff game or beat top-10 opponents? The Rose Bowl silenced all that, coming from behind to beat the vaunted Crimson Tide in overtime.

And now, finally, the ultimate prize, a national title. There was no backing in. No lucky draws. Michigan played the toughest teams in the nation and beat them all.

As for the controversies?

"We're innocent," Harbaugh said, volunteering this at his postgame news conference before he was even asked, "and we stood strong and tall because we're innocent ... these guys (the players) are innocent. ... And it went exactly as we wanted it to go."

His critics might doubt him, but no doubt countless Michigan fans around the world were saying the same thing. It went the way they wanted it to go. From the first victory of the season to that final Sainristil pick, a classic image, one young man, gripping a football and running down the field in such a once-in-a-lifetime victorious moment that he couldn't breathe when it was all over. But then, that's what happens when all Hail breaks loose.

his love for his missing head coach, and Corum sticking a rose in his teeth when the Wolverines slammed the door shut on Alabama out in Pasadena.

It was a year of highlights and headlines, the latter often eclipsing the former. And in the center of the storm was always Harbaugh, kicking up dust clouds as if auditioning to play Pig Pen in the Peanuts cartoon.

But if Harbaugh stands accused of creating unneeded noise around this program, he must be credited with silencing some of the loudest criticisms that have followed him and the Wolverines for years.

Can't beat Ohio State? Forget that. Loses to the

THE SEASON 11

Champions of the West ... East, North & South — here are the stories of the Wolverines' first 11 national titles.

CROWNING
ACHIEVEMENTS

1901

11-0 (4-0 WESTERN)

▶▶▶ **COACH:** Fielding Yost. ▶▶▶ **CAPTAIN:** Hugh White.
▶▶▶ **ROSE BOWL:** Michigan 49, Stanford 0.

NOTEWORTHY: Fielding (Hurry Up) Yost's first team at Michigan set the tone for a national powerhouse in the early 1900s. The Wolverines finished 11-0 and outscored opponents, 550-0. In Yost's first five seasons, Michigan went 55-1-1 and outscored opponents, 2,821-42 (an average score of 49.5 to 0.7). In Yost's first game, the Wolverines toyed with Albion, 50-0. A month later, they destroyed Buffalo, 128-0 — at a time when TDs were worth only five points, as were field goals, and the forward pass was illegal. In its four Western Conference games — Indiana, Northwestern, Chicago and Iowa — U-M outscored the enemy, 134-0. The season's closest contest was 28-0 at Ohio State, which wouldn't join the conference until 1912 as its ninth member. (At that time, U-M was in the middle of its 1907-17 hiatus from the Western, to become commonly known as the Big Ten upon its return. The conference lists its birthdate as Feb. 8, 1896, with seven members — U-M, Chicago, Illinois, Minnesota, Northwestern, Purdue and Wisconsin — and its birthplace as the Palmer House hotel in Chicago.) Although 4-0 in the Western, U-M shared the conference title with Wisconsin (2-0) because the standings were based on winning percentage. Yost went to Ann Arbor from Stanford, where he coached in 1900 before a rule that only alumni could lead its teams. His first season at Michigan ended with a 49-0 victory over Stanford at the Tournament of Roses in Pasadena, California, now considered the first bowl ever played. "The 49-0 score speaks for itself," the *Free Press* reported. "It caps a season that will be long remembered in college football history." The NCAA recognizes U-M as the national champion, although Harvard (12-0) also lays claim to it. The first wire service poll did not arrive until 1936; before then, numerous organizations — including Helms, named for a Los Angeles bakery — and publications selected their top teams, some considered more legit than others, depending on whom one rooted for. The NCAA also considered mathematical formulas that were applied retroactively over the decades.

Fielding Yost
DETROIT FREE PRESS ARCHIVES

1902

11-0 (5-0 WESTERN)

▶▶▶ **COACH:** Fielding Yost.

▶▶▶ **CAPTAIN:** Harrison (Boss) Weeks.

NOTEWORTHY: Fielding Yost's second "Point-a-Minute" team picked up right where the first left off, outscoring opponents, 644-12, and capturing another national championship. In his first game (and U-M's second over-all) with Michigan Agriculture, the Wolverines beat the future Michigan State, 119-0, as Al Hernstein scored seven touchdowns, two more than the "modern era" school record set by Ron Johnson in 1968. (Hassan Haskins, against Ohio State in 2021, and Blake Corum, against Connecticut in 2022, matched Johnson's five TDs, also all on the ground.) The Wolverines reached triple digits again for home-coming, 107-0 over Iowa. However, Yost's defense finally yielded its first points — 48-6 against Case in its second game and 23-6 against Minnesota in its finale on Thanksgiving. Coverage of the Gophers game produced the big headline on the front of the next day's *Free Press*: "MAIZE AND BLUE WAVES TRIUMPHANT IN WEST." For the first time since 1898, the Wolverines won the Western outright (outscoring its five foes, 217-6). The *Free Press* reported: "Minnesota introduced its mascot, 'Doc Knipe,' the bulldog that has been announced before the contest, parad-ing him at the head of its brass band, a uniformed organization of 40 pieces. Michigan produced a rival mascot in the form of a live turkey, its wings dyed blue, its other plumage a bright yellow. It proved, ultimately, to be Turkey Day in a double sense."

1903

11-0-1 (3-0-1 WESTERN)

▶▶▶ **COACH:** Fielding Yost.

▶▶▶ **CAPTAIN:** Curtis Redden.

NOTEWORTHY: Michigan's third straight national championship, according to the NCAA, was shared with Princeton (11-0). Once again, the Yostmen — a common newspaper term for U-M on second reference — were a ruthless machine that steamrolled opponents, 565-6. However, those six points scored by Minnesota, with two min-utes left in Minneapolis, led to a 6-6 tie and a shared Western title. The *Free Press* reported that the late touch-down "brought a premature close this afternoon when thousands of Gopher rooters swarmed onto the playing field, making it impossible to continue play." The tie was the only time that Fielding Yost did not win in his first 56 games at U-M, a 50-month stretch from 1901-05. Plus, Michigan left behind an earthen-ware water jug, which the teams played for when they met again in 1909. (U-M won, 15-6.) Thus was born the Little Brown Jug rivalry. The Wolverines "only" outscored their four conference oppo-nents, 101-6. Michigan's brightest star was All-America halfback Willie Heston, a scoring machine elected to the College Football Hall of Fame in 1954. He made All-America again in 1904 and finished his U-M career with 72 touch-downs. Considered Yost's first recruit, Heston played for three years at San Jose Normal, including against Stanford when Yost was its coach in 1900. Earlier that year, Yost was Normal's coach, but he left for Stanford without coaching a game. Yost, also a lawyer, convinced Heston, already 22 years old, to join him at Michigan and to study law. Because of the loose eligibility rules at the time, Heston played four more seasons. Eventually, he became a lawyer in Detroit, an assistant prosecutor and a judge.

1904

10-0 (2-0 WESTERN)

▶▶▶ **COACH:** Fielding Yost.

▶▶▶ **CAPTAIN:** Willie Heston.

NOTEWORTHY: Michigan achieved its fourth straight national championship — imagine Fielding Yost's salary if he were coaching in the 2020s! — but the rest of the Midwest appeared to be catching up with the Wolverines. The NCAA considers it a shared title with another future Ivy Leaguer, Penn (12-0). Michigan allowed six points to Ohio State (in a 31-6 victory), was held to 28 points by Wisconsin (in a 28-0 victory) and allowed 12 points to Chicago (in a 22-12 victory), en route to sharing the Western title with Minnesota (13-0, 3-0). The finale with Chicago was only the third game in Yost's four seasons decided by fewer than two touchdowns — following the 6-6 tie with Minnesota in 1903 and a 6-0 victory over Wisconsin in 1902. Still, U-M outscored oppo-nents, 567-22, and there were a pair of 72-0 results and a 95-0 triumph over Kalamazoo. Plus, with a 130-0 destruc-tion, Yost showed no mercy to West Virginia, his home state and where he played during law school. In that game, the most lopsided in U-M history, John Curtis and Fred Norcross each scored five touchdowns. Norcross, a quarter-back, scored on runs of 45, 52 and 27 yards and two 80-yard kick returns. Along with its 22 TDs, U-M gained 1,500 yards, according to press reports. The *Free Press* wrote: "Yost took the varsity team to task last night. He told them that they were loafing, and that the old men were the worst offenders. ... Each had taken a firm resolve to show today that he could play football in Yost style." Yost's championship streak ended the next season when he lost for the first time in the season's final game, 2-0 at Chicago. At that point, Yost was 55-1-1 at U-M — a .974 win percentage. An annual section in the football media guide points out that during the five-season unbeaten streak, excluding losses to U-M, the winning percentage of its 56 opponents was .695, 44 of the 56 finished with winning records and six would have had undefeated seasons.

1918

5-0 (2-0 BIG TEN)

▶▶▶ **COACH:** Fielding Yost.

▶▶▶ **CAPTAIN:** Tad Wieman.

NOTEWORTHY: If only 2021 could have matched 1918, a pandemic-stricken season that ended with a two-score victory over Ohio State (14-0) ... and then a national championship. Michigan Agricultural, yet to be rebranded Michigan State or to be allowed in the Big Ten, was the only team to score on Michigan, in its second season back in the conference after a 10-year absence. U-M had departed because of "reforms" instituted by the Western Conference, including a five-game limit and three years of eligibility. Also at that time, Stanford's president accused U-M of "professionalism" in *Collier's* magazine and Yost of recruiting "expert players" who weren't true students. In 1918, the Wolverines shared the national championship with Pittsburgh, according to the NCAA, and shared the Big Ten title with Illinois (5-2, 4-0) and Purdue (3-3, 1-0). In its coverage of the Ohio State game, the schools' first as Big Ten members, the *Free Press* banner headline read: "Michigan Averts Disaster in Final Period, Scoring Twice, Winning 14-0." Its deck headline, even though passing had been legal since 1906, pointed out: "FIRST TOUCHDOWN FOLLOWS BLOCKED KICK, OTHER IS ON FORWARD PASS, AFTER PENALTY PUTS O.S.U. CLOSE TO OWN GOAL." The *Free Press* reported that after the game, Yost caught the earliest train from Columbus to Cincinnati for a connection to Nashville. "That means that the last vestige of hope for an Illinois game is gone, and also that the Nebraska challenge will be ignored," the paper wrote. "So far as Yost is concerned, the season is ended. And when it ends for him, it ends for Michigan." Fullback Frank (Stek) Steketee, noted for his skill as a line-plunger, placekicker and punter, became Michigan's 13th All-America.

1923

8-0 (4-0 BIG TEN)

▶▶▶ **COACH:** Fielding Yost.

▶▶▶ **CAPTAIN:** Harry Kipke.

NOTEWORTHY: To win his sixth and final national championship, Fielding Yost's Wolverines did it the hard way, with conference victories over Iowa, Wisconsin and Minnesota by a combined 19 points. U-M still beat Ohio State by 23 points and outscored its foes, 150-12. Michigan and Illinois (8-0, 5-0) shared the Big Ten title. And, according to the NCAA, the Wolverines and Fighting Illini shared the national title, too. After a 0-0 tie at Vanderbilt the previous season, to Yost's protégé and brother-in-law, Dan McGugin, the Wolverines won, 3-0, at Ferry Field. It was the Commodores' first loss in three seasons. One of the *Free Press* headlines read: "OBSTINATE DEFENSE HOLDS BACK YOSTMEN." U-M ended the season with 10-0 victory over undefeated Minnesota that led the *Free Press* to report: "Michigan played smarter football. Michigan fought harder. Michigan out-thought Minnesota." U-M's biggest star was halfback Harry Kipke, an All-America, a future Hall of Famer, a future MSU and U-M coach and a future U-M regent. Against the Golden Gophers, Kipke, also a fantastic punter, connected on a 37-yard dropkick. He earned nine letters in football, basketball and baseball. Yost added athletic director to his duties in 1921, stepped down as football coach after the 1923 championship but returned with back-to-back Big Ten titles in 1925 and '26 before stepping down again. He remained the athletic director until 1941, five years before his death at 75.

Harry Kipke

1932

8-0 (6-0 BIG TEN)

▶▶▶ **COACH:** Harry Kipke.

▶▶▶ **CAPTAIN:** Ivan Williamson.

NOTEWORTHY: After Fielding Yost stepped down a second time, a former guard and captain, Tad Wieman, went 6-2 and 3-4-1 in 1927-28, although Yost apparently more than dabbled with the team. Yost then turned to Harry Kipke, the hero of his last national champion who had gone 3-4-1 in his lone season as a head coach. That was at Michigan State in 1928 and included a 3-0 loss to Michigan. After a 5-3-1 record in his first season, Kipke won four straight Big Ten titles, the last two years adding national titles. Only Yost and Bo Schembechler also won four straight conference titles at U-M. Kipke's first national title became U-M's seventh (and most dubious). The Wolverines, though, were a Yost-like powerhouse, outscoring opponents, 123-13. The season opened with a 26-0 victory over MSU, especially significant because the previous two seasons the teams had played to scoreless ties. The season ended with a 3-0 victory at Minnesota. Michigan lays claim to the national title although the NCAA recognizes Southern Cal as the sole champion. The Trojans (10-0) received the nod from the majority of publications and organizations. The Wolverines' top endorsement came from Parke Davis, a player at Princeton in the 1890s and a national championship-winning coach at Lafayette who in 1933, a year before his death, selected champions from 1869 to 1932. He used no special formula, just looked at schedules, trusted his knowledge and used his gut. For 1923, Davis decided on a tie at the top among U-M, USC and Colgate (9-0). (For 1928, which the NCAA recognizes Georgia Tech, Davis picked Tech and the University of Detroit as his champions.) The Wolverines shared the Big Ten title with Purdue (7-0-1, 5-0-1). Their All-Americas were center Charles Bernard, end Ted Petoskey and quarterback Harry Newman, who scored 57 of U-M's 83 points in Big Ten play and who won the Douglas Fairbanks Award, which predated and briefly overlapped with the Heisman for the country's top player.

1933

7-0-1 (5-0-1 Big Ten)

▶▶▶ **COACH:** Harry Kipke.

▶▶▶ **CAPTAIN:** Stanley Fay.

NOTEWORTHY: Despite a scoreless, late-season tie with Minnesota, Michigan captured its eighth national championship with minimal debate. The NCAA recognizes only the Wolverines as the champ. Shortly before his death, Parke Davis, though, wrote that the title should be shared by Michigan and Princeton, his alma mater. The Tigers went 9-0 with seven shutouts in their second season under coach Fritz Crisler. What really didn't make sense, once again, was that the Wolverines shared the Big Ten title with the Golden Gophers. The conference continued to decide its champion based on winning percentage; the Wolverines and Gophers batted 1.000 but Minnesota's conference record consisted of two victories and four ties. Overall, the Gophers were 4-0-4. Michigan outscored opponents, 131-18, recording five shutouts and surrendering only 2.3 points a game. U-M's All-Americas were center Charles Bernard, end Ted Petoskey and tackle Francis (Whitey) Wistert. Pro coaches called Bernard the country's top player, equally good on offense and defense. "Without Bernard," Associated Press sports editor Alan Gould said, "the Wolverines could hardly have topped the toughest league in the country." Wistert became the first of three All-America brothers at U-M, with Albert (1942) and Alvin (1948-49) to come. All were inducted into the College Football Hall of Fame. A right-handed pitcher, Whitey was the top baseball player in the Big Ten and briefly pitched for the Cincinnati Reds in 1934. He helped coach U-M before practicing law in industrial relations.

1947

10-0 (6-0 Big Nine)

▶▶▶ **COACH:** Fritz Crisler.

▶▶▶ **CAPTAIN:** Bruce Hilkene.

▶▶▶ **ROSE BOWL:** Michigan 49, Southern Cal 0.

NOTEWORTHY: After his back-to-back national titles, Harry Kipke suffered a pair of 1-7 and a pair of 4-4 seasons. In 1938, Herbert Orin (Fritz) Crisler took the reins after a successful six-year run at Princeton (35-9-5). Crisler was an innovator on and off the field. He implemented the winged helmet in 1938 to help quarterbacks find their receivers, and it became an iconic symbol for the program. As athletic director from 1941-68, he expanded Michigan Stadium to be the country's largest college stadium. His biography on the College Football Hall of Fame's website starts with these two sentences: "Fritz Crisler, the father of two-platoon football, was an unruffled, self-possessed individual who directed his teams with a quietly forceful drama that rivaled a military commander. His buck lateral and spinner offense was the most dazzling in football and required Swiss-watch precision, hair-breadth timing and flawless faking." His first nine teams went 61-16-3 (.781) with seven top-10 finishes in the AP poll but only one Big Ten title, in 1943. His single wing offense helped Tom Harmon win the 1940 Heisman. In 1947, his final season on the sideline, Crisler's Mad Magicians posted a 9-0 regular season, outscored opponents, 394-53, and routed USC, 49-0, in the Rose Bowl, U-M's first bowl since the initial Pasadena game on Jan. 1, 1902. Halfbacks Bob Chappuis and Bump Elliott, whose careers were interrupted by World War II, were the All-Americas on a team of stars. Chappuis finished second in the Heisman voting; Elliott led the Big Nine with 54 points and was selected its MVP by the *Chicago Tribune*. Still, the Wolverines were behind No. 1 Notre Dame (9-0) in the final AP poll. After the Rose Bowl, in an unprecedented move, the AP polled sportswriters to decide whether the Wolverines or Irish should be No. 1. U-M won handily. However, the NCAA — and the AP — recognizes Notre Dame as the national champion.

1948

9-0 (6-0 Big Nine)

▶▶▶ **COACH:** Bennie Oosterbaan.

▶▶▶ **CAPTAIN:** Dominic Tomasi.

NOTEWORTHY: Content to be just the athletic director at age 49, Fritz Crisler promoted his top assistant, Bennie Oosterbaan, in early 1948. Oosterbaan had been one of the greatest athletes in Big Ten history. As an end, he was U-M's first three-time All-America and was selected to the all-time All-America team in 1951. He also was an All-America in basketball and all-conference in baseball. With QB Benny Friedman, also later inducted into the College Football Hall of Fame, they became such an effective passing combination they changed the entire sport. At times, it was called "The Benny-to-Bennie Show." After graduation, Oosterbaan eschewed pro baseball and football offers to coach at U-M, which he did in all three sports. Ranked fourth in mid-October, the Wolverines moved to No. 1 with a 28-0 victory over No. 3 Northwestern. When they slipped back to No. 2 in early November, they returned to No. 1 with a 35-0 victory over Navy. A 13-3 triumph at Ohio State closed out the season (U-M was ineligible for the Rose Bowl because of a no-repeat rule) and secured a 10th national title. Notre Dame finished second. U-M's three All-Americas were an eclectic trio. His career interrupted by WWII, Dick Rifenburg returned from the Navy to become the country's second-highest scoring end. QB Pete Elliott arrived in 1945 as a Navy trainee, left as the only Wolverine to win 12 letters — in football, basketball and golf — and later became the director of the Pro Football Hall of Fame. Tackle Alvin (Moose) Wistert dropped out of high school, worked in a factory and enlisted in the Marines. After the war, determined to follow in his brother's footsteps, Wistert passed a high school equivalence test, enrolled at Boston University using the G.I. bill and played as a 30-year-old freshman. He transferred to Michigan and, like his brothers Francis (aka Whitey) and Albert (aka Ox), played tackle and wore No. 11. He made All-America in 1948 and again in 1949 at age 33.

1997

12-0 (8-0 Big Ten)

▶▶▶ **COACH:** Lloyd Carr.

▶▶▶ **CAPTAINS:** Jon Jansen, Eric Mayes.

▶▶▶ **ROSE BOWL:** Michigan 21, Washington State 16.

NOTEWORTHY: Perfection! Nearly a half-century after its last national championship, Michigan ran the table for its 11th. Following four straight four-loss seasons — a pair each with Gary Moeller and then Lloyd Carr as the coach — the Wolverines posted their first season without a loss or a tie since 1948. Cornerback Charles Woodson became the first primarily defensive player to win the Heisman Trophy, easily outdistancing Tennessee quarterback Peyton Manning, a result that still rankled fans from the Volunteer State. The Wolverines started the season No. 14, reached the top of the Associated Press media poll in mid-November and added the No. 1 ranking in the ESPN/ *USA TODAY* coaches poll in late November. Despite a 21-16 victory over No. 8 Washington State in the Rose Bowl, the Wolverines were forced to share the national championship with Nebraska after a controversial flip-flop by coaches, a result that still rankled Wolverine Nation. U-M won the AP vote decisively; Nebraska (13-0) edged U-M in the coaches poll on the strength of a 42-17 victory over No. 3 Tennessee in the Orange Bowl. Five days before the season, Carr picked a fifth-year senior and former walk-on, Brian Griese, as his quarterback over 1996's starter, Scott Dreisbach, and a redshirt sophomore, Tom Brady. U-M opened with a 27-3 demolition of Colorado, a popular choice as a national title contender. With Notre Dame in the red zone pursuing a tying touchdown late in a 21-14 game, U-M stopped running back Autry Denson on second-and-three, third-and-two and fourth-and-a-yard-and-a-half. Iowa led, 21-7, at the half after three Griese interceptions; Griese then threw two touchdown passes and scored on a fourth-and-goal sneak for a 28-24 victory. At Happy Valley, U-M's 34-8 thrashing of No. 2 Penn State marked Joe Paterno's worst home loss in 32 years as coach and lifted U-M to the top of the AP poll. Against No. 4 Ohio State, Woodson set up the game's first TD with a 37-yard reception, scored the game's second TD with a 78-yard punt return and made an end-zone interception in the third quarter of a 20-14 victory. Throughout the season, in which he picked off eight passes and recorded touchdowns rushing, receiving and returning, Woodson never hesitated each Saturday to tell everyone he was the best college football player in America. The only Wolverines to win the Heisman had been halfback Tom Harmon in 1940 and wide receiver/returner Desmond Howard in 1991. Woodson, overcome with emotion during the Heisman ceremony, dropped to one knee and covered his face. "My body just shut down," he said. "I didn't really think I'd win it. I almost broke down, and I'm not a crier." But his mother, Georgia Woodson, gave a different view of her son, who had to wear leg braces until age four: "Oh, he had tears in his eyes. Charles doesn't cry very often, but he's always been a very sensitive boy." For what it's worth, the National Football Foundation and Football Writers Association of America selected the Wolverines as their No. 1 team.

Charles Woodson pointed the way on one of the most iconic front pages in the Detroit Free Press' 193-year history.
DETROIT FREE PRESS

Offensive tackle and captain Jon Jansen, a fourth-year junior from Clawson, was as light as a rose in the hands of the Michigan faithful as thousands celebrated a victory over the Buckeyes, an undisputed Big Ten championship and a trip to Pasadena.

2

THE SEASON

Two straight disappointing finishes provided the motivation — it was time to go to work for a third East crown, another Big Ten title and, of course, another shot at the big Blue prize.

A Michigan captain, Mike Sainristil decided to return for a fifth season for emotional moments such as touching the Big House's iconic banner before the opener against ECU.
JUNFU HAN/DETROIT FREE PRESS

THREE FOR ALL

KIRTHMON F. DOZIER/DETROIT FREE PRESS

After throwing two pick-sixes in the 2022 semifinals, quarterback J.J. McCarthy forced himself to watch Texas Christian's celebration for future motivation. He did the same thing after Georgia's rout in the 2021 semifinals ended his freshman season.

The road to the 2023 CFP championship began with a stunning loss and a wild offseason for the Wolverines.

By Gene Myers

On Michigan's final offensive play of the 2022 season, on a fourth-and-10 with 35 seconds left, the Rimington Trophy winner as the country's best center snapped the ball prematurely, and it struck the stomach of the Wolverines' best all-around quarterback in at least a generation. "An ugly last play for Michigan" came the call from ESPN's Sean McDonough.

Instead of his usual "enthusiasm unknown to mankind" persona, coach Jim Harbaugh was a forlorn figure after TCU's victory at the Fiesta Bowl. "There's a lot of things we could have done better," he rued at his postgame news conference.
KIRBY LEE/ USA TODAY SPORTS

Michigan's second straight trip to the College Football Playoff again ended in the semifinals. In 2021, the Wolverines were routed by Georgia, 34-11, and the Bulldogs went on to win the title. This time, the heartache was greater, a 51-45 loss to Texas Christian at the Fiesta Bowl. No longer the overachieving underdog, U-M was a 7½-point favorite and TCU the Cinderella. But the Horned Frogs turned the game into a shootout against a vaunted defense. U-M's J.J. McCarthy threw for 343 yards and two touchdowns — but also two interceptions that the Frogs turned into pick-sixes.

The *Detroit Free Press* wrote that U-M coach Jim Harbaugh "looked shocked afterwards, his face and his stare vacant." The center, Olusegun Oluwatimi, solemnly called his mistake "a brain fart." As for the quarterback?

"We'll be back," McCarthy said. "And I promise that."

The Wolverines did make it back to the College Football Playoff for a third straight season, the first Big Ten team to do so. They again beat Michigan State, Penn State and Ohio State, previously accomplished only in 2000 and 1997. They again won the Big Ten championship game, which made Harbaugh the first coach to win three consecutive outright titles in the league's 127-year history. They again were 13-0, but

MARK J. REBILAS/USA TODAY SPORTS
Co-offensive coordinator Matt Weiss arrived from the Baltimore Ravens in 2021 only to be fired while under investigation for possible computer access crimes at Schembechler Hall two years later.

this time seeded No. 1 for the CFP tournament and ranked No. 1 in the media and coaches polls. It was U-M's first top ranking since 1997, when the Wolverines captured a share of the national championship with Lloyd Carr as coach.

But before all that came an eight-month offseason of chaos and controversy. It started with another NFL flirtation by Harbaugh and ended after athletic director Warde Manuel suspended

him for the opening three games. Along the way were allegations of computer crimes at Schembechler Hall and NCAA violations during the COVID-19 pandemic, the firing of a coordinator, the nearly simultaneous arrival and exit of Shemy Schembechler, Bo's son, and the constant speculation about a longer, more generous contract for Harbaugh, who was in the NCAA's crosshairs for supposedly lying to its investigators.

The angst started on Jan. 1, 2023, with a report that the Denver Broncos had reached out to Harbaugh about their coaching vacancy. Soon after, Harbaugh talked with the owner of the Carolina Panthers.

Only 11 months earlier, Harbaugh interviewed with the Minnesota Vikings on national signing day for college football teams — before returning without an offer. He told the *Free Press* that he informed Manuel his dalliance with the

NFL was a "one-time thing" and "will not be a recurring theme every year." Then he signed a new contract for the second straight offseason, which more than restored cuts that halved his salary after his 2-4 record in 2020's COVID-19 season.

A date emerged that should live in infamy for the football program. On Jan. 5, a U-M employee told campus police that "computer access crimes" occurred at Schembechler Hall during the early signing period right before Christmas. Also, Harbaugh released a statement saying he expected to stay, but "no one knows what the future holds." And then the NCAA sent a draft notice of allegations of football improprieties, four low-level infractions but a high-level charge against Harbaugh.

Soon after, Harbaugh held a virtual interview with the Broncos. But on Jan. 16, U-M's first-year president, Santa Ono — not Manuel — tweeted that Harbaugh would return for his ninth season. Harbaugh declared in a tweet: "I once heard a wise man say, 'Don't try to out-happy, happy.'" Plus, the *Free Press* reported another contract renegotiation was in the works.

The next day, ESPN broke the news that Matt Weiss, co-offensive coordinator and quarterbacks coach, had been placed on leave for possible

computer crimes. Three days later, Manuel announced the Weiss had been fired "after a review of University policies" but revealed nothing else. Eventually, the *Detroit News* obtained Weiss' termination letter, which said because he did not appear for a meeting or offer additional information, U-M had no choice but to conclude he "inappropriately assessed the computer accounts of other individuals."

No arrests were made or charges brought in 2023, although the *Free Press* reported in late October that the FBI had partnered with U-M police for several months in its investigation, which the department called an "utmost priority."

On Twitter, before it became known as X, Weiss wrote: "The potential of Team 144 knows no bounds."

Harbaugh turned the offense over to co-offensive coordinator Sherrone Moore as the sole coordinator and play-caller. Moore also was to continue coaching the offensive line, which for back-to-back seasons had won the Joe Moore Award as the country's best. To coach the quarterbacks, Harbaugh promoted Kirk Campbell, 36, who had spent the last season in an off-the-field role as an analyst after two years as Old Dominion's offensive coordinator.

The rest of the staff: Jesse Minter, defensive coordinator;

JUNFU HAN/DFP

A football player for Bo Schembechler, Warde Manuel became Michigan's athletic director in 2016. Even in the best of times, Manuel rarely fielded questions from the media. During the turmoil of 2023, he communicated by releasing statement after statement.

JUNFU HAN/DETROIT FREE PRESS

During his first suspension, Jim Harbaugh elected to rotate the role of acting head coach to his top lieutenants. From top to bottom: Jesse Minter, Jay Harbaugh, Mike Hart and Sherrone Moore.

The first family of Michigan football — Millie, Shemy and Bo — posed before leaving for the 1981 Rose Bowl. Winless in his five previous trips to Pasadena, Bo Schembechler beat Washington, 23-6.
DAVID C. TURNLEY/DETROIT FREE PRESS

Jay Harbaugh, special teams coordinator and safeties coach; Grant Newsome, tight ends; Mike Hart, running backs; Ron Bellamy, wide receivers; Steve Clinkscale, co-defensive coordinator and cornerbacks; Mike Elston, defensive line and recruiting coordinator; and Chris Partridge, linebackers.

According to the NCAA, the Wolverines committed four Level II violations, by definition deemed "more than a minimal but less than a substantial or extensive recruiting, competitive or other advantage." Eventually, Michigan did not contest these violations dating to 2021, in which coaches contacted recruits during a COVID-19 dead period, analysts served in on-field capacities and coaches watched players work out via a video feed.

The NCAA also accused Harbaugh of a Level I violation, by definition a "severe breach of conduct" that "seriously undermines or threatens the integrity of the NCAA collegiate model." The NCAA concluded that Harbaugh lied to or misled its investigators about the Level II violations. Harbaugh refused to admit any wrongdoing.

Citing and following NCAA policy, Harbaugh didn't say much about the NCAA's investigation as winter turned to spring and spring turned to summer. When spring practice started in February, he said: "Compare us to perfect, and we're going to come up short. ... Compare us to any other program, it doesn't get any better." At the Big Ten media days in July, he

JUNFU HAN/DFP
An offensive lineman for Jim Harbaugh until a serious injury, Grant Newsome rose through the ranks at U-M from student assistant coach to graduate assistant coach to tight ends coach.

said: "I'd love to lay it all out there. Nothing to be ashamed of."

The NCAA's enforcement staff and U-M's athletic department negotiated a settlement that called for a four-game suspension for Harbaugh, one-game suspensions for Moore and Newsome, and a one-year show-cause penalty for former defensive coordinator Mike Macdonald, now the DC for the Baltimore Ravens. But in August the NCAA's Committee on Infractions rejected the deal. That likely ensured the case was headed to a full hearing before the committee and would not be concluded before 2024.

With the opener less than two weeks away, Manuel admitted publicly for the first time that misdeeds were committed and announced that Harbaugh would be suspended for the opening three games, although he could coach during the week. Moore and Newsome were suspended for one game.

Harbaugh said in a statement: "I will continue to do what I always do and what I always tell our players and my kids at home, 'Don't get bitter, get better.'"

Unclear was whether Manuel (and presumably Ono) unilaterally decided to suspend Harbaugh or whether the coach was involved in the process. U-M hoped its preemptive strike would avoid or lessen additional NCAA sanctions in the future.

To serve as acting head coach during the nonconference season, Harbaugh selected Minter for the opener against East Carolina, Jay Harbaugh, Jim's son, for the first half and Hart for the second half against UNLV, and Moore for Bowling Green.

Back in May, Glenn (Shemy) Schembechler, son of the legendary coach, announced on social media that he had been hired as assistant director of recruiting. He was out of a job three days later.

Schembechler, 53, had a long football resume: graduate assistant and recruiting assistant in the early 1990s for U-M coach Gary Moeller and two decades as an NFL scout for several teams. But he also had scores of posts

THE SEASON 23

In early February 2023 at the Crisler Center, during a basketball game against Nebraska, several football players received a rousing ovation walking across court during a break in the action. Tailback Blake Corum asked in advance for a few moments with a microphone — and he made headlines by telling fans that Michigan would win the national championship and go down in history.

and likes on Twitter that could be considered racist, transphobic, insensitive and offensive. Among them were claims that slavery and Jim Crow laws benefited Blacks, criticism of House minority leader Hakeem Jeffries with African tribal imagery, praise for longshot presidential candidate Robert Kennedy Jr. "as long as he doesn't go trans," and conspiracy theories about Black Lives Matter, the Jan. 6 Capitol insurrection and the 2020 presidential election.

Harbaugh and Manuel released a joint statement that Schembechler had resigned and apologized that his social media activity "caused con-

cern and pain for individuals in our community." Schembechler filed a lengthy mea culpa via a public relations and crisis firm in Arizona, saying he was disappointed by his "flippant behavior on Twitter" and apologizing to "the Black community, all communities."

In June, Harbaugh said that U-M dumped the company that vetted Schembechler before he was hired. "I've known Shemy for a long time," Harbaugh said, "but there's no sacred cows."

Despite all the accusations, investigations and firings from the TCU loss to the opener against East Carolina, the Wolverines during the offseason smartly bolstered

Defensive lineman Kris Jenkins paid no attention to temperatures in the low 20s as he arrived at Michigan Stadium for the annual slugfest with Ohio State. It got to 35 by the noon kickoff.

their roster and wholly embraced a win-it-all-now, us-against-the-world mentality from the top down.

At halftime of a basketball game, tailback Blake Corum told the fans at the Crisler Center: "Man, it feels good to be back! We're gonna win the national championship and go down in history. That's all I got."

The Wolverines lost nine players to the NFL draft — only Alabama and Georgia sent more players to the pros with 10 draftees each. Defensive tackle Mazi Smith went in the first round, followed by tight end Luke Schoonmaker (second), cornerback DJ Turner (second), placekicker Jake Moody (third), defensive end Mike Morris (fifth), center Olusegun Oluwatimi (fifth), punter Brad Robbins (sixth), offensive lineman Ryan Hayes (seventh) and wide receiver Ronnie Bell (seventh).

But nine starters from the 2022 team who could have entered the NFL draft opted to return and formed the heart-and-soul of the Wolverines. They did so to bolster their draft stocks and to chase a championship, swayed to one degree or another by Name, Image and Likeness opportunities and the crowdfunding One More Year Fund. The nine included the top running back (Corum), the top offensive lineman (Zak Zinter), the top defensive lineman (Kris Jenkins) and the leader of the secondary (Mike Sainristil).

The Wolverines' six captains, selected in August by a team vote, came from this veteran group: linebacker Michael Barrett, offensive guard Trevor Keegan, Corum, Jenkins, Sainristil and Zinter.

In the transfer portal, the Wolverines once again gained more than they lost. The big-name departures were quarterback Cade McNamara, who lost his job to McCarthy, and tight end Erick All, who lost his job to Schoonmaker. They landed at Iowa. Others to leave included wide receivers A.J. Henning (to Northwestern) and Andrel Anthony (to Oklahoma), defensive back RJ Moten (to Florida) and edge Taylor Upshaw (to Colorado and then Arizona).

The Wolverines added nine transfers, all of whom played vital roles: center Drake Nugent, Stanford; offensive tackle Myles Hinton, Stanford; offensive tackle LaDarius Henderson, Arizona State; cornerback Josh Wallace, Massachusetts; linebacker Ernest Hausmann, Nebraska; edge Josaiah Stewart, Coastal Carolina; tight end AJ Barner, Indiana; kicker James Turner, Louisville; and quarterback Jack Tuttle, Indiana.

In July, the media members who covered the Big Ten selected Michigan as the overwhelming favorite to win the conference title for a third straight season. That marked the first time since 2019 that Ohio State hadn't been the choice in the annual poll conducted by cleveland.com.

Harbaugh's contract negotiations, although started in January, continued to drag on. He did not relish the media's repeated questions about it.

The August polls pegged Michigan as the country's second-best team, behind two-time defending champion Georgia. It was the Wolverines' highest preseason ranking since also being No. 2 in 1991.

With a quarterback he called a "once-in-a-generation type of guy," a team vibe he described as "vibrant ... infectious," a staff, team and fan base fixated on a national championship, and eight wild-and-crazy months since the TCU game finally in the rearview mirror, Harbaugh felt confident and prepared for the task ahead. He just wished he could be on the sidelines at the Big House on the season's first three Saturdays.

"I've heard people comment it's a slap on the wrist," he said. "It's more like a baseball bat to the kneecaps or to the shoulder."

ROBERT GODDIN/USA TODAY SPORTS

At the Big Ten media days, Jim Harbaugh cracked a smile and made a plea to the inquiring crowd of sportswriters. "Keep me in the realm of what I know," he said, "which is football."

THE CRYSTAL BALLS

BIG TEN: How the media expected the Big Ten season to unfold in the annual poll conducted by cleveland.com.

EAST DIVISION	WEST DIVISION
1. Michigan	1. Wisconsin
2. Ohio State	2. Iowa
3. Penn State	3. Minnesota
4. Maryland	4. Illinois
5. Michigan State	5. Nebraska
6. Rutgers	6. Purdue
7. Indiana	7. Northwestern

CHAMPIONSHIP GAME: Michigan over Wisconsin

US LBM COACHES POLL: In the preseason coaches poll, the Wolverines were ranked second but received none of the 66 first-place votes. Those went to Georgia (61), Alabama (4) and Ohio State (1).

1. Georgia	14. Utah
2. Michigan	15. Oregon
3. Alabama	16. Texas Christian
4. Ohio State	17. Kansas State
5. Louisiana State	18. Oregon State
6. Southern Cal	19. Oklahoma
7. Penn State	20. North Carolina
8. Florida State	21. Wisconsin
9. Clemson	22. Mississippi
10. Tennessee	23. Tulane
11. Washington	24. Texas Tech
12. Texas	25. Texas A&M
13. Notre Dame	

The Wolverines set sail with a full wind and the verve of a pirate, thanks to J.J. McCarthy and Roman Wilson.

JUNFU HAN/DETROIT FREE PRESS

With Ronnie Bell off to the NFL, J.J. McCarthy needed a new favorite receiver for his junior season. For openers, he hit it off well with Roman Wilson, a senior from Maui. They hooked up six times for 78 yards and three touchdowns against East Carolina. "That man right there is one of the most special players in the country," McCarthy said, pointing two seats to his left at the postgame news conference.

Walk the plank

By Rainer Sabin

THE BIG PICTURE

J.J. McCarthy remembers what it was like in 2022, impeded by the obstacles placed in front of him. First, he dealt with the uncertainty spawned by a shoulder injury, which slowed his offseason development entering his sophomore year. Then he endured a tense quarterback competition with team captain Cade McNamara, which wasn't resolved until after the second game. When it ended with McCarthy named the starter, he immediately was tasked with running a restrictive offense that favored its prolific ground attack.

"There was just a lot of resistance, a lot of stuff to push through," he recalled.

That was no longer the case. McCarthy felt liberated, a rising star freed from the shackles of confining game plans.

In his 2023 debut, a 30-3 romp over East Carolina, McCarthy powered the Wolverines. He threw 30 times, produced 26 completions, 280 passing yards and three touchdown strikes. It was a sublime performance that tickled the imaginations of fans who yearned for the former five-star recruit to be unleashed.

McCarthy wanted this, too. In many ways, McCarthy's ambitions far exceeded those of his coach, Jim Harbaugh, who was content with pounding teams into oblivion, leaning on a rugged ground attack that spawned a sudden revival in 2021. The effective formula combined a formidable offensive line with a pair of talented running backs to poison the opposition. It yielded great results, leading to 25 victories in 28 games the past two seasons.

But it lost its potency in the College Football Playoff, where the Wolverines fell to Georgia and TCU in games that highlighted the necessity of having a versatile offense and a quarterback like McCarthy at its controls.

Even Harbaugh arrived at that conclusion during the offseason, when he repeatedly mentioned his desire for greater balance and a more robust passing game. "I want to be 50-50," he said on Michigan's in-house radio show earlier in the week. "I really do."

So, there was McCarthy distributing the ball all over the field in the opener, sending it into tight windows, zipping it from one side of the field to the other and dropping it into pockets between defenders. He was surgical as he carved up the Pirates, engineering five straight scoring drives during a bountiful period that spanned the first and third quarters. As acting head coach Jesse Minter said, the scintillating play was a continuation of what took place in practice.

Last month, during preseason camp, Minter approached McCarthy and told him he

J.J. McCarthy fired 30 passes, and running backs coach Mike Hart pointed out U-M ran the ball 31 times. "At the end of the day you want to be a 50-50 offense, right?" Hart said.
JUNFU HAN/DFP

had never been around a more consistent player and leader.

It was his dependability, Minter said after the blowout, that "leads to performances like that." The hard evidence compiled against ECU approached perfection, highlighted by McCarthy's 86.7 completion percentage and 198.1 passer rating. Only Elvis Grbac's 90.9 percentage (20-for-22) against Notre Dame in 1991 topped McCarthy's effort in U-M history.

But perhaps what stood out most of all was, by the time he exited late in the third quarter, McCarthy had thrown the ball six more times than U-M had run it.

Was that the goal of Kirk Campbell, the quarterbacks coach who made the play calls while Harbaugh and offensive coordinator Sherrone Moore served suspensions? Or was it the byproduct of a defense hell-bent on stopping the run?

To McCarthy, it didn't really matter. "It's very nice, selfishly as a quarterback, you know what I mean?" he said.

THE PLAY-BY-PLAY

▶▶▶ After a first-quarter interception by Mike Sainristil, in his second season since moving from receiver to nickelback, the Wolverines' scored the season's first points on a 14-yard McCarthy to Roman Wilson pass on third-and-nine. They reconnected for a 10-yard TD in the second quarter and a 15-yard TD in the third.

▶▶▶ In his return from a severe meniscus tear, Blake Corum ran for 73 yards on 10 yards, including 21- and 37-yard runs and a two-yarder for a TD. But his backfield buddy, Donovan Edwards, lacked his usual burst and struggled for 37 yards on 12 carries.

▶▶▶ Five offensive and five defensive starters from the Fiesta Bowl started against East Carolina. Two other starters, defensive backs Will Johnson and Rod Moore, were out with injuries. Three transfers started: center Drake Nugent, offensive tackle Myles Hinton and cornerback Josh Wallace. A fourth transfer, sophomore linebacker Ernest Hausmann from Nebraska, led the defense with six tackles.

Besides his usual pre-game ritual of meditating on the field to free his mind, J.J. McCarthy longed to free his coach from the shackles of a three-game, school-imposed suspension. JUNFU HAN/ DETROIT FREE PRESS

THE PREAMBLE

▶▶▶ Because of suspensions imposed by athletic director Warde Manuel for minor NCAA violations, coach Jim Harbaugh (out for three games) watched the opener against a 35½-point underdog from the home of offensive coordinator Sherrone Moore (out for one). "His wife, Kelli, made some sandwiches, his two daughters were there, and my son Johnny," Harbaugh said two days later. "We had a good time."

▶▶▶ As a tribute to his missing coach, J.J. McCarthy wore a maize-and-blue shirt with HARBAUGH and his old number on the front. McCarthy affixed a piece of white tape with the handwritten word FREE. In the first quarter, he orchestrated the offense as it lined up single file on a hash-mark and each player held up four fingers. Harbaugh had used that train formation early in his U-M tenure against Wisconsin and wore No. 4 as a U-M quarterback in the 1980s.

THE PRESS BOX

▶▶▶ **RAINER SABIN, DETROIT FREE PRESS:** "Michigan showed why cupcake games to open the season can be beneficial if the right approach is taken. This year, the Wolverines used the opener to expand the dimensions of their offense and improve an area — the passing game — that was underdeveloped last year."

▶▶▶ **AUSTIN MEEK, THE ATHLETIC:** "Sherrone Moore, apparently a Peacock subscriber, hosted what had to be Saturday's weirdest Michigan football watch party."

▶▶▶ **SHAWN WINDSOR, DETROIT FREE PRESS:** "Was McCarthy protesting his own school? Nah, he was protesting the absurdity of a system that forced his school to self-impose a suspension. Mostly, though, he just wanted his coach back."

THE PRIME NUMBER

313

East Carolina's streak of consecutive games in which it scored, extended because of a 33-yard field goal on the final play. The Pirates last were shut out on Oct. 4, 1997, a 56-0 wipeout by Syracuse.

JUNFU HAN/DETROIT FREE PRESS

During his son's suspension, Jack Harbaugh agreed to serve as an assistant head coach. He also lent a staffer a hand with the equipment after the game. No job too big, no job too small!

JUNFU HAN/DETROIT FREE PRESS

After bolting between two East Carolina defenders, Roman Wilson hauled in his third touchdown catch — a 15-yarder in the third quarter. The last Wolverine with three receiving TDs in a game was Nico Collins at Indiana in November 2019.

THE PROCLAMATIONS

▶▶▶ **TAILBACK BLAKE CORUM:** "If we really wanted to, we probably could've tried to get over 100 yards, me or Donovan (Edwards) or any of the other running backs. But why? When we've got guys like Roman (Wilson) and J.J. (McCarthy), they can just slang that thing."

▶▶▶ **COACH JIM HARBAUGH:** "I felt the love from them just doing them. I could see it in our players. I could see it in our coaches. And that's what I want them to do. I want them to do them. 'Be you' is the way we say around here. I saw them having fun."

JUNFU HAN/DETROIT FREE PRESS

In his first game since knee surgery ended his 2022 season, Blake Corum locked his eyes on a pylon prize. "It just felt great being back out there," he said. "It was kind of like a warmup."

THE POLLS

▶▶▶ The top four in the US LBM coaches poll remained unchanged as the teams won by a combined 157-20 score. No. 5 LSU lost to No. 8 Florida State, 45-24, in a passing duel for the ages. FSU's Jordan Travis: 342 yards, four TDs. LSU's Jayden Daniels: 346 yards, one TD.

RK	TEAM	W-L	PVS
1.	Georgia	1-0	1
2.	Michigan	1-0	2
3.	Alabama	1-0	3
4.	Ohio State	1-0	4
5.	Florida State	1-0	8

▶▶▶ In the AP media poll, the order was Georgia, Michigan, Alabama, FSU, OSU.

U-M's passing game was more than enough to deal out UNLV, but the run game was folding at all the wrong times.

JUNFU HAN/DETROIT FREE PRESS

Blake Corum, a senior from Marshall, Virginia, dashed through a gaping hole for a first down en route to 80 rushing yards and three touchdowns. Still, he wasn't pleased. "Feel like I could've done more with what I was given," he said. "I'm always hard on myself."

House rules

By Tony Garcia
THE BIG PICTURE

Whether sitting on Sherrone Moore's couch or his own, Jim Harbaugh loved much of what he had seen from his Wolverines during his suspension.

The electric passing game led by J.J. McCarthy and Roman Wilson. The defense that hadn't surrendered a point with its two-deep on the field. The coaching staff shuffling around to make the beginning of an abnormal season feel as normal as possible.

The Rebels kept Donovan Edwards tied up like a pretzel. A junior from West Bloomfield, Edwards eked out only nine yards in six carries. He did better as a receiver: five catches for 26 yards.
JUNFU HAN/ DETROIT FREE PRESS

In some ways, the head coach couldn't ask for anything more. "It's darn near a walk in the park to coach these guys," Harbaugh said two days after Michigan's 35-7 victory over UNLV.

That said, if he were going to ask for something more, it would be for Michigan's run game to look like, well, Michigan's run game.

The Wolverines ranked No. 53 in the nation in rushing, averaging 150.5 yards through two games. A year earlier, they were No. 10 and averaged 251 yards.

So what gives? It's not health — even though Blake Corum had knee surgery and Donovan Edwards needed a broken thumb repaired and rehab from a partially torn patella tendon. Mike Hart, the running backs coach who served as acting head coach for the second half against UNLV, said Corum and Edwards were "100 percent."

"The thing I'm looking at is the inefficient plays," Harbaugh said. "They're outnum-

JUNFU HAN/DETROIT FREE PRESS

Donovan Edwards (No. 7) and Blake Corum (No. 2) warmed up for UNLV expecting to have breakout afternoons on the ground. Didn't happen. Still, U-M rushed for 179 yards.

bering the efficient runs."

By Harbaugh's definition, inefficient plays on the ground go for three yards or fewer, anything from four to nine yards was efficient, and a run that went for at least 10 yards was explosive.

Against UNLV, Corum ran 15 times for 80 yards and three touchdowns, but had just two explosive runs, an 11-yard run up the middle on third-and-seven in the first quarter and a 19-yard scamper in the third quarter. His other 13 carriers netted 50 yards, five of which the staff deemed inefficient.

Edwards struggled even more. He ran six times for nine yards — five inefficient rushes and one carry that netted four yards. For the season, Edwards had 18 rushes for 46 yards, just two explosive plays and 12 inefficient plays.

"It's a combination of everybody," Harbaugh said. "We've got to block on the perimeter, we got to get the safeties better blocked by our wide receivers. Tight ends are really playing well, offensive line, yeah, it's we're missing a guy here or it's one guy on a play.

"And running backs, when I say a guy here a guy there, it's a missed cut here or a missed cut there. But it's something we're very focused on and emphasizing."

The less-than-stellar numbers were surprising, given that U-M returned perhaps the country's most decorated backfield and four players who started at least half-a-dozen games on 2022's Joe Moore Award-winning offensive line.

In case that wasn't enough, U-M brought in three more starters from Power Five teams up front, two of whom (Drake Nugent and LaDarius Henderson) had been captains.

But, as Sherrone Moore pointed out, chemistry didn't happen overnight.

"When you have new guys in there, that's something that's going to happen (over time)," said Moore, the offensive coordinator who also coached the O-line. "I always tell them, 'We do this all together.' So I'm not gonna put the blame on them and say it's just the players."

Moore then listed his starters, for now, left to right: Karsen Barnhart, Trevor Keegan, Nugent, Zak Zinter and Myles Hinton. The backups: Henderson, Giovanni El-Hadi, Greg Crippen, Jeff Persi and Trente Jones.

THE PREAMBLE

▶▶▶ Coach Jim Harbaugh spent the middle game of his three-game suspension by working the chain gang during son Jack's youth football game and then watching his Wolverines, this time 36½-point favorites, from the comfort of his home. Offensive coordinator Sherrone Moore, instead of sharing sandwiches with his boss, returned from his one-game suspension and oversaw an awesome aerial attack but an "inefficient" run game.

▶▶▶ Special teams coordinator Jay Harbaugh, Jim's oldest son, and running backs coach Mike Hart each spent a half as the acting head coach. U-M led, 21-0, after Harbaugh's half; U-M outscored UNLV, 14-7, in Hart's half. Hart became the first Black man and seventh former Wolverine to serve as head coach. The Rebels were so manhandled that with 8:17 left in the game they had amassed only 148 yards — 11 rushing and 137 passing — but avoided a shutout with a nine-play, 81-yard drive (50 rushing, 31 passing).

JUNFU HAN/DETROIT FREE PRESS

Mike Hart's historic half as acting head coach led to a postgame chat with Jenny Dell of CBS and a postgame news conference in which he thanked Jim Harbough for the opportunity.

THE PLAY-BY-PLAY

▶▶▶ J.J. McCarthy completed his first 13 passes en route to another nearly flawless three-quarter performance. He finished 22-for-25 passing for 278 yards and two touchdowns and ran three times for 38 yards. His 88.0 completion percentage topped his 86.7 percentage (26-for-30) in the opener.

▶▶▶ McCarthy's TD passes went to Roman Wilson. In fact, they had combined for all five of the team's TD passes thus far. The first against UNLV, a 13-yarder with 24 seconds left in the first half, produced a 21-0 lead. The second, 4:29 into the third quarter, put the game away. McCarthy had written "47" with a black marker on the back of his left hand, a tribute to Ryan Keeler, a friend since childhood and his left tackle in 2018 on their Class 7A state championship team in Illinois. Keeler, a defensive lineman at UNLV who wore No. 47, died of an undetected heart condition in February 2023. McCarthy's second TD pass to Wilson covered 47 yards. "If that's not God," McCarthy said, "I don't know what it is."

▶▶▶ After no sacks and little pressure in the opener, U-M's defense devastated the Rebels, recording five sacks in the defense's first 20 plays. A pair of sophomore defensive tackles were terrors: Mason Graham had five tackles, 1½ for a loss, a half-sack and a forced fumble; Kenneth Grant had four tackles, 2½ for a loss, 1½ sacks and a tipped pass.

Roman Wilson caught four passes for 89 yards with TDs of 47 and 13 yards. But afterward he was more excited about a block of his. "I'll give up a touchdown," he said, "to get another pancake any day." After two games, Wilson had 10 catches for 167 yards and five TDs.
JUNFU HAN/DETROIT FREE PRESS

JUNFU HAN/DETROIT FREE PRESS

THE PRIME NUMBER

87.3

J.J. McCarthy's completion percentage after two games (48 of 55 for 558 yards and five touchdowns), tied for the third-highest percentage in NCAA history after two games.

With nearly as many touchdown passes (five) as incompletions (seven) for the season, J.J. McCarthy admitted, "I feel like all aspects of my game improved this offseason."

THE PRESS BOX

▶▶▶ **RAINER SABIN, DETROIT FREE PRESS:** "The Wolverines repeatedly invaded UNLV's backfield and turned quarterback Doug Brumfield into a human pinata. The pressure was applied from everywhere, as a mix of blitzes from the second and third levels freed up the defensive line to do some damage."

▶▶▶ **TONY GARCIA, DETROIT FREE PRESS:** "If there's one single aspect of the 2023 season that's the most surprising, it's Donovan Edwards' slow start. Edwards was shut down again, touching the ball 11 times for just 35 yards."

Forget three yards and a cloud of dust. When linebacker Michael Barrett tackled Jacob De Jesus after a short pass, it was five yards and a cloud of rubber pellets. Barrett made a team-high four solo tackles.
JUNFU HAN/DETROIT FREE PRESS

THE PROCLAMATIONS

▶▶▶ **EDGE RUSHER JAYLEN HARRELL:** "Everyone eats in this defense. ... It was a good showing, just gotta keep stacking days and weeks."

▶▶▶ **COACH JIM HARBAUGH:** "J.J. is phenomenal. So on fire, so on point. ... The kind of throws he's making, too, they're NFL-caliber throws into tight windows. The accuracy is off the charts. I mean, he's putting balls six inches in front of the number."

THE POLLS

▶▶▶ Alabama's 34-24 home loss to Texas jumbled the Top 10 in the US LBM Coaches Poll. The Tide fell from third to 10th, and the Longhorns jumped from 10th to sixth.

RK	TEAM	W-L	PVS
1.	Georgia	2-0	1
2.	Michigan	2-0	2
3.	Florida State	2-0	5
4.	Ohio State	2-0	4
5.	Southern Cal	3-0	6

▶▶▶ In the AP poll, Michigan and Georgia remained 1-2, followed by FSU (up one), Texas (up seven), USC (up one) and OSU (down one). Alabama stood 10th.

What should have been a sleeper under the lights at the Big House was a showcase of the Wolverines' early issues.

JUNFU HAN/DETROIT FREE PRESS

On a long ball late in the first half, Tyler Morris couldn't stretch out far enough. J.J. McCarthy, after two weeks of pinpoint accuracy, completed eight of 13 passes, but three went to the wrong team. "I'm always gonna move on," he said, "and stay in the present moment."

Falcon stressed

By Tony Garcia
THE BIG PICTURE

With a talent advantage over Bowling Green in every facet of the game, Michigan primarily wanted a clean performance under the Big House lights heading into Big Ten play.

It got quite the opposite.

The Wolverines turned the ball over three times in the first half, and four times total, including three interceptions by J.J. McCarthy, all inside the red zone. They led by a single point late in the first half, 7-6, before taking a 14-6 halftime lead. When the offense went three-and-out to start the second half, more than a few of the 109,955 fans feared the threat of a monumental upset.

But by then the Falcons, 40½-point underdogs, were down to their third-string quarterback. On their first play of the half, edge rusher Jaylen Harrell's pressure on a screen pass led to Kris Jenkins' interception at the BGSU 11. He rumbled to the 2 — "too fat to finish the play strong," the 305-pound defensive

tackle joked — and Blake Corum scored on the next play for a 21-6 lead.

Two plays into BGSU's next drive, Harrell knocked the ball free as Hayden Timosciek tried to pass, and Michael Barrett recovered. A 42-yard James Turner field goal followed for a 24-6 lead.

After a BGSU three-and-out, a flea-flicker featuring McCarthy, Corum and Cornelius Johnson ended with a circus catch on a tipped ball, a 50-yard touchdown and a 31-6 lead.

Seventeen points in less than 6½ minutes ended the threat of a horrible loss but not Michigan's miserable night. McCarthy's next pass — which would be his last — became interception No. 3. After completing 87.3 percent

of his passes in the first two games, McCarthy finished a dismal 8-for-13 passing for 143 yards, two touchdowns and three interceptions (his first picks of the young season).

"I'm going to take all of those on the chin, put them all on me," McCarthy said. "A lot of stuff just obviously didn't go my way, the offense's way. But I just can't wait to watch the tape and see the mistakes that were made."

His weren't the only mistakes. The first-team offense had not turned over the ball all season. The running game stalled at times after a fast start. Twice U-M fumbled short kickoffs, recovering one and losing one that led to a BGSU field goal. Two sec-

ond-quarter field goals were the first points surrendered by the first-team defense. Transfer defensive back Josh Wallace was burned on a double move but the Falcons receiver dropped a wide-open pass in the end zone.

In the *Free Press* report card, the offense and coaches received D+ grades and this comment: "In a game with a talent mismatch like this, half the job is showing up, and Michigan did not do that for the majority of the contest."

Johnson caught three passes for 71 yards. Roman Wilson caught only two for 42, but that included a 33-yarder for his sixth touchdown.

Perhaps the best news was that Corum looked like a returning All-America. He opened the night with a 54-yard run and finished with his first 100-yard performance of the season: 12 carries for 101 yards.

Still, U-M's running game struggles didn't appear completely solved. The Wolverines ran 27 times for just 92 yards after the game's opening series — when U-M picked up 77 yards on four rushes. Donovan Edwards broke off nice 11- and 10-yard runs but struggled for 29 yards in his other seven carries.

"We moved the line of scrimmage very well, thought those guys up front took to the challenge that we gave to them this week," acting head coach Sherrone Moore said. "I think overall from a run-game standpoint we definitely improved."

Offensive coordinator Sherrone Moore batted cleanup in the order of Jim Harbaugh stand-ins. "Being the head coach was exciting," said Moore, also the offensive line coach.

THE PREAMBLE

▶▶▶ Fans at the Big House likely knew more about Bowling Green coach Scot Loeffler than they did U-M's latest acting coach, Sherrone Moore, the offensive coordinator. Loeffler was a hotshot quarterback recruit in the mid-1990s before a shoulder injury. He started coaching for U-M as a student, no small contributor to Lloyd Carr's 1997 national championship team. Then he was a graduate assistant and Carr's QB coach for six years. In four years he turned a BGSU program in ashes into a bowl participant. Still, the Falcons, at 1-1, were 40½-point underdogs for the last game of Jim Harbaugh's suspension.

▶▶▶ Ties abounded between U-M and BGSU. Jack and Jackie Harbaugh, Jim's parents, met at Bowling Green, and Jack was an assistant there when Jim entered elementary school. During his weekly radio show, Jim Harbaugh sang Ay Ziggy Zoomba, the Falcons' fight song, and said his father insisted they would "come up here and kick your ass." During the suspension, Jack, at 84, served as an associate head coach. Jim knew Loeffler well. Among Loeffler's roommates from his playing days was Mike Elston, U-M's defensive line coach.

Poor Camden Orth. Usually the backup quarterback, Orth moved Bowling Green effectively even with Wolverines such as Mike Sainristil pursuing him with a vengeance. Orth, though, didn't make it to halftime before suffering a concussion.

THE PLAY-BY-PLAY

▶▶▶ Michigan's first drive of the game flashbacked to the 2021 and 2022 seasons, when the Wolverines owned a lethal ground attack and their offensive line won the Joe Moore Award as the best in the land. On first down from the U-M 23, Corum ripped off a 54-yard counter run — the longest play of the season. Edwards followed with an 11-yard run on a reverse to the BGSU 12. McCarthy ran left for eight yards. Then Corum pounded his way through the middle for a four-yard touchdown. In four plays, U-M covered 77 yards in 112 seconds.

▶▶▶ None of Michigan's five scoring drives lasted longer than 2:42. The five drives required 17 plays (possessions of four, five, one, four and three plays).

▶▶▶ Bowling Green managed only 205 yards — 96 before quarterback Camden Orth's second-quarter exit with a concussion and 79 in two garbage-time drives.

THE PRIME NUMBER

1

Touchdowns through three games not scored by Blake Corum (six rushing TDs) or Roman Wilson (six receiving TDs). Cornelius Johnson, a fifth-year wide receiver, broke their scoring stranglehold with a 50-yard TD reception from McCarthy with 6:28 left in the third quarter.

Blake Corum looked more and more like Vintage Blake Corum. With 101 yards, he cracked the 100-yard mark for the first time since his knee surgery. Plus, the offensive line stepped it up. "From a run-game standpoint," Sherrone Moore said, "we definitely improved." KIRTHMON F. DOZIER/ DETROIT FREE PRESS

THE PROCLAMATIONS

▶▶▶ **QUARTERBACK J.J. MCCARTHY:** "When I was struggling and I came to the sideline, everybody was trying to pick me up. We have a team full of leaders that have each other's back, and that's something truly special."

▶▶▶ **TAILBACK BLAKE CORUM:** "Of course we're excited to get Coach Harbaugh back. I know he's fired up, he can't wait."

THE PRESS BOX

▶▶▶ **TONY GARCIA, DETROIT FREE PRESS:** "Finally, the nonconference slate is over. ... Can anybody say they had a lot of fun during these three games, other than the tailgating?"

▶▶▶ **RYAN FORD, DETROIT FREE PRESS:** "The Wolverines had 77 yards rushing on their first drive and 92 the rest of the way? Didn't realize the UAW called a standup strike at the Big House."

▶▶▶ **AUSTIN MEEK, THE ATHLETIC:** "Don't let the final score fool you: Michigan's 31-6 victory against Bowling Green was anything but an easy tune-up for Big Ten play."

KIRTHMON F. DOZIER/DETROIT FREE PRESS

A 50-yard flea-flicker for a touchdown to Cornelius Johnson livened up a ho-hum third quarter. Johnson showed great hands after Davon Ferguson deflected the pass. That said, Ferguson nearly made it four interceptions for J.J. McCarthy.

THE POLLS

▶▶▶ The top nine teams in the US LBM coaches poll remained the same. But No. 10 Alabama slipped to 12th after struggling past South Florida, 17-3.

RK	TEAM	W-L	PVS
1.	Georgia	3-0	1
2.	Michigan	3-0	2
3.	Florida State	3-0	3
4.	Ohio State	3-0	4
5.	Southern Cal	3-0	5

▶▶▶ In the AP media poll, Alabama fell from 10th to 13th. The top five: Georgia, Michigan, Texas, FSU and USC.

What busted coverage? With one play, Mike Sainristil flipped the momentum for U-M — and earned a souvenir.

On an amazing 71-yard interception return for a touchdown, Mike Sainristil never was touched by a Scarlet Knight. But he ran into teammate Junior Colson, sent him flying through the air and somehow turned upfield and zigzagged his way to the end zone.
KIRTHMON F. DOZIER/ DETROIT FREE PRESS

Buff enough

By Tony Garcia
THE BIG PICTURE

With the Turnover Buffs resting on his face, Mike Sainristil raised his hands as he blew kisses to the 109,756 fans for homecoming at Michigan Stadium.

He had made amends.

On the opening possession, Sainristil, a fifth-year nickelback, fell down in man-to-man pass coverage, which resulted in a 69-yard Rutgers touchdown exactly one minute in. No matter. With Rutgers down 10 and facing fourth-and-two deep in U-M territory in the third quarter, Sainristil got it back.

The band finally was back together. His three-game suspension over, coach Jim Harbaugh returned to the sideline and celebrated the good times with Blake Corum (No. 2), Mike Sainristil (No. 0) and Fredrick Moore (No. 3), a freshman receiver.

Sainristil watched the wide receiver screen develop, jumped the route and took the interception 71 yards the other way for a touchdown, which proved to be the defining moment in Michigan's 31-7 victory.

"Good players make mistakes," Sainristil said. "He scored a touchdown, but I kind of brushed it off right away and said (to the defense), 'I'm gonna get y'all one back.'"

"That's a difference-maker," coach Jim Harbaugh said. "The guy that makes the magic happen when you need the magic to happen."

Cornerback Will Johnson introduced Turnover Buffs during the 2022 season to celebrate a turnover by the defense. Protocol dictated that a player who snared an interception or recovered a fumble rushed to the sideline to don a pair of Cartier sun-glasses, known as Buffs. Then his defensive teammates surrounded him, and a photograph was taken to mark the joyous occasion.

While Michigan's defense, again, sparked the victory, the offense had plenty of positives in the Big Ten opener. The Wolverines' offensive and defensive lines so dominated Rutgers that Harbaugh channeled Bo Schembechler's words, declaring Michigan was "grinding some meat."

Quarterback J.J. McCarthy showed the turnover worries that surfaced against Bowling Green could be forgotten, at least for now. The Scarlet Knights, who entered with five interceptions, had none at the Big House; McCarthy completed 15 of 21 passes for 214 yards and a touchdown. He was also more active in the ground game then he had been, running seven times for 51 yards.

"J.J., I mean he's tough to defend," Harbaugh said. "Can throw the ball in the pocket, throw the ball out of the pocket, really accurate thrower, can get the ball to any part of the field. And he's super-athletic. Had 214 yards throwing, 50-some running; that's a lot of production by the quarterback position — when we needed it."

It also kept the defense's attention on him, which helped open the rushing attack. Blake Corum ran 21 times for 97 yards and two touchdowns, and U-M gained 201 yards on 40 carries — five yards a pop.

Rutgers, meanwhile, was stonewalled on the ground. One week after running through Virginia Tech for 256 yards (at the pace of 7.5 yards a carry), the Scarlet Knights were held to 77 yards on 23 carries. Kyle Monangai, the conference's leading rusher, gained only 27 yards on 11 carries.

"That's a run wall," Harbaugh said. "That's big boy football."

Afterward, Harbaugh was downright giddy at his first postgame news conference since his three-game suspension. Rainer Sabin wrote in the *Free Press* that Harbaugh was "as effervescent as he has ever been" and "seemed buzzed by the high level of competition, intoxicated by the thrill of victory." Harbaugh delivered one-liners, praised his players, bantered with his father and mimicked Schembechler.

"Everybody kept saying, 'Welcome back, welcome back,'" Harbaugh said. "I never really left, but I wasn't where I was supposed to be. ...

"Coach wanted it, but the players wanted it even more. You could tell. It was great."

KIRTHMON F. DOZIER/DETROIT FREE PRESS

It was just like old times for J.J. McCarthy with Jim Harbaugh back on the sideline. McCarthy produced 214 yards in the air and 51 yards on the ground. "That's a lot of production by the quarterback position," Harbaugh said, "and when we needed it."

THE PREAMBLE

▶▶▶ With his three-game suspension over, Jim Harbaugh was fired up at his Monday news conference before the Big Ten opener against Rutgers. His players said it, media observers confirmed it. "I went to a place I've never been, which wasn't on the sideline," he said. "Seeing the game in a different way, through a different lens, I think it's made me a better coach." Then, with few specifics, he revealed he would "implement some new things that I haven't done as it relates to a few new policies around here to make sure I don't ever get sidelined again." He called it "ramping up to a gold standard."

▶▶▶ The Scarlet Knights owned a 3-0 record and a growing reputation for stout line play. They had the 16th-best rushing offense (210.7 yards a game) and the 15th-best rushing defense (70.3). But the Knights also had started 3-0 the past two seasons, only to finish 5-8 in 2021 and 4-8 in 2022, and their passing game was sorely lacking, ranked 121st in the country. "We bully bullies," tailback Blake Corum would say later. "We take pride in that."

THE PRIME NUMBER

75

Victories at Michigan by Jim Harbaugh. The milestone came in his 100th game. The only coaches to do so quicker were Fielding Yost (83 games), Bo Schembechler (88) and Lloyd Carr (98).

THE PLAY-BY-PLAY

▶▶▶ Michigan had not allowed an opponent to score first or reach the end zone before the fourth quarter. Soon after Rutgers scored 60 seconds into the game, the Wolverines launched their drive of the season — seven plays that featured rugged runs and pinpoint passing and covered 94 yards. It included a reverse flea-flicker: J.J. McCarthy handed to Corum, who pitched to Donovan Edwards, who pitched back to McCarthy, who had all the time in the world to find tight end Colston Loveland wide open for 35 yards. On the next play, Corum scored on a two-yard run.

▶▶▶ Michigan took a 14-7 lead late in the first half with an 11-play, 79-yard drive that lasted nearly six minutes and again showed off the offense's diversity. McCarthy hit freshman Semaj Morgan with an 18-yard TD pass.

▶▶▶ The Wolverines ended the game with another epic drive, holding the ball for 10 plays that ate up the final 6:57.

Indiana transfer AJ Barner had one catch after three weeks. Against Rutgers, he caught three passes for 13 yards. In Week 2, he made his first start when U-M began with a two-tight end set. KIRTHMON F. DOZIER/DFP

THE PRESS BOX

▶▶▶ **RAINER SABIN, DETROIT FREE PRESS:** "J.J. McCarthy looked like a different QB, demonstrating poise in the pocket as he singed the Scarlet Knights' defense with his arm and legs."

▶▶▶ **SHAWN WINDSOR, DETROIT FREE PRESS:** "Look, U-M was supposed to beat Rutgers. But few expected this sort of dominant performance, not against a team that's traditionally hard to dominate. What does it say? That Corum is coming. That McCarthy, when asked, can make plays on the ground, and that those plays should unlock everything else. That their tight end, Loveland, already looks like a high-round draft pick. That their defense is as fast as it has been in a while. And that they need their head coach. When he's on the sideline, the team is different."

THE POLLS

▶▶▶ Ohio State passed Florida State in the US LBM coaches poll on the strength of its 17-14 victory over Notre Dame. Texas and Southern Cal traded Nos. 5 and 6.

RK	TEAM	W-L	PVS
1.	Georgia	4-0	1
2.	Michigan	4-0	2
3.	Ohio State	4-0	4
4.	Florida State	4-0	3
5.	Texas	4-0	6

▶▶▶ In the AP media poll, USC fell from fifth to eighth because of a close call with lowly Arizona State. The top six: Georgia, Michigan, Texas, OSU, FSU and Penn State.

THE PROCLAMATIONS

▶▶▶ **TAILBACK BLAKE CORUM:** "He just brings the juice. I wish you could've seen him in the locker room, it was great. And just hearing his speech before we hit the field today, it was great as well. We love Coach Harbaugh, and it was great just having him back on the sideline with us."

▶▶▶ **RUTGERS COACH GREG SCHIANO:** "They're a very good football team. You have to make sure you are on point with everything. Because if you're not, it's not just a gain — it's a touchdown. If you're not, it's not just a PBU (pass broken up) — it's a pick-six."

▶▶▶ **LINEBACKER JUNIOR COLSON:** "At the end of the day, there can't be two smash mouths and we were the first ones. So we had to go out and dominate up front. You gotta show 'em who's boss."

It wasn't exactly a welcome mat for the Wolverines' first road trip, but the defense walked all over the Cornhuskers.

DYLAN WIDGER/USA TODAY SPORTS

Linebacker Michael Barrett did his part to ensure that quarterback Heinrich Haarberg would not become the first native Nebraskan to win his first three career starts since Eric Crouch, who later won the Heisman Trophy in 2001. Haarberg was sacked four times.

Red carpet

By Tony Garcia

THE BIG PICTURE

S ince 1996, for 343 consecutive games, the seventh-longest streak in major-college history, the Nebraska Cornhuskers had at least scored a few points. They had not been shut out at home since 1968, the season before a young assistant named Tom Osborne was promoted to offensive coordinator, installed the I formation and reignited the golden age of Huskers football started by head coach Bob Devaney.

On a third-and-one, Michigan turned to its 239-pound batting ram to power his way to a first down. U-M got more than that: Kalel Mullings ran 20 yards for a 14-0 lead halfway through the opening quarter.

When Michigan deflected Nebraska's first pass high in the air, all 339 pounds of defensive tackle Kenneth Grant somehow made an over-the-shoulder interception in traffic and stuck the landing.

Michigan nearly ended both streaks as its defense suffocated a vaunted Nebraska ground attack and bullied the Huskers' offensive line. But with little more than four minutes left in the game, Michigan's third-string defense slipped up for one play: Josh Fleeks, a senior transfer from Baylor just recently converted from receiver to running back, dashed through the middle for 74 yards and the end zone.

Outside of that, the defense was flawless on a steamy 96-degree afternoon in Michigan's first road game of the season. On offense, the once-struggling rushing attack ran over, through and around Nebraska's run defense — ranked No. 2 in the country at 46.3 yards a game — for 249 yards and three touchdowns.

Add it all up and No. 2 Michigan steamrolled Nebraska, 45-7. The Wolverines had no turnovers, a TD catch for the ages, a huge interception by a gargantuan D-lineman, a fourth-and-one stuff and no penalties. But how did that rank among coach Jim Harbaugh's list of complete games?

"Pretty darn high," he said. "The guys did a tremendous job, just so focused on their football. It was an important task, critical that we come in here on the road and play good football.

"Our guys did that and then some, in all phases."

Under new coach Matt Rhule, the Cornhuskers hadn't allowed more than 60 rushing yards in splitting their first four games. But when U-M's senior battering ram, Kalel Mullings, scampered for a 20-yard touchdown less than eight minutes into the first quarter, the Wolverines had 67 rushing yards and a 14-0 lead.

From there, the Wolverines used a distributed rushing attack to keep the Cornhuskers off-balance: Four ballcarriers — Mullings, Blake Corum, Donovan Edwards and J.J. McCarthy — had at least 30 yards at halftime. U-M led, 28-0.

"Can't start a game better than we did," Harbaugh said.

Corum led the way, finishing with 16 carries for 74 yards and one touchdown, his ninth of the season, all five yards or fewer. McCarthy scored on a 21-yard run and completed 12 of 16 passes for 156 yards and two touchdowns, each to Roman Wilson.

"We have the best O-line in the country," Mullings said. "No ifs, ands or buts about it."

Michigan's defense lived up to its statistical billing. It entered the game first in scoring defense (5.8 points a game), first in total defense (231.5 yards) and 13th in rushing defense (80.5). The Wolverines recorded four sacks, five pass breakups, two forced fumbles and an interception. Previously averaging 234.8 yards on the ground, the Cornhuskers ran 16 times for 39 yards — 2.4 a carry — for the three quarters U-M's starters played.

"You hate these kind of losses," Ruhle said. "They all count the same, but they hurt when you have this type of loss."

It was Nebraska's 14th straight loss against a top-five opponent.

"You look over at their sideline and see them deflated," said U-M edge rusher Braiden McGregor. "It's awesome."

THE PREAMBLE

▶▶▶ The Wolverines were installed as 18½-point favorites for their first road game. Nebraska boasted a new coach, Matt Ruhle, the successor to former Cornhuskers quarterback Scott Frost, a lowly 16-31 in four-plus seasons and 5-20 in one-score games, but still loathed by Michigan fans because of his lobbying that helped Big Red earn a share of the 1997 national title. Previously, Ruhle quickly resurrected teams at Temple and Baylor.

▶▶▶ Before arriving in Lincoln, Ruhle didn't last three seasons after jumping to the NFL with the Carolina Panthers, going 11-27. In 2023, despite a stout rushing defense and strong running game, his Huskers opened with losses to Minnesota and Colorado before beating Northern Illinois and Louisiana Tech. Before the U-M game, Ruhle said he looked at Jim Harbaugh and his program as a model on how to rebuild the Cornhuskers.

Welcome to the Big Ten! Jim Harbaugh chatted up Nebraska's Matt Ruhle before lowering the boom. **DYLAN WIDGER/ USA TODAY SPORTS**

THE PLAY-BY-PLAY

▶▶▶ For the first time all season, Michigan started with the ball. From its 25, U-M methodically overpowered the Huskers until the 11th play, from the Nebraska 29, when J.J. McCarthy fired a laser into the wind for Roman Wilson in the end zone. An outstretched safety nearly tipped the ball. As Wilson leaped with his back to the end line, safety Isaac Gifford, with his back to the play, also leaped and planted his helmet against Wilson's chest. Somehow, Wilson reached around Gifford's head, caught the pass with two hands and pinned the ball against Gifford's helmet. Their feet landed in the end zone, and Wilson's butt landed beyond the line end with Gifford on top of him. Wilson still had the ball. "I could see it clear as day, went up and grabbed it," Wilson said. "The dude's head was between me and the ball. I'm not going to let go of the ball, so I just brought it down with me."

▶▶▶ On Nebraska's second play, edge rusher Braiden McGregor deflected a pass high into the air. In a scrum near the line of scrimmage, defensive tackle Kenneth Grant, a 339-pound sophomore, made an over-the-shoulder interception. The offense needed three plays to go 29 yards and convert the turnover into seven points and a 14-0 lead.

▶▶▶ To build a 28-0 halftime lead, U-M scored

DYLAN WIDGER/USA TODAY SPORTS

J.J. McCarthy dashed 21 yards for a TD and a 21-0 lead. "It was nice looking over to The Boneyard," he said of Nebraska's student section, "and seeing three-quarters of it gone by halftime."

on a 21-yard McCarthy run, completing an 88-yard drive, and a 16-yard reception by Wilson, coming with 23 seconds on the clock.

THE PROCLAMATIONS

▶▶▶ **COACH JIM HARBAUGH:** "They're not arrogant. You should see the way they practice, the way they go about their business. ... There's zero entitlement, and I think they're attacking everything they do. They want it. They want to earn it the old-fashioned way."

▶▶▶ **HARBAUGH AGAIN:** "The gravitational force of the Earth is tremendous. And so are some of the forces against a football team — some of the things that are sent there to divide a football team. And the ones that aren't divided are playing in the playoffs and eventually champion."

THE PRESS BOX

▶▶▶ **AMIE JUST, LINCOLN (NEBRASKA) JOURNAL STAR:** "There was a lot to loathe from Nebraska's side of this. The Huskers were outplayed in every single facet of the game. If I were to write on everything that looked bad for Nebraska, I'd have a short novel."

▶▶▶ **RAINER SABIN, DETROIT FREE PRESS:** "Once again, the Wolverines came to an opponent's field, saw an inferior squad lined up across from them and then conquered them swiftly. *Veni, vidi, vici.*"

THE POLLS

▶▶▶ With a 40-14 victory over No. 24 Kansas, Texas moved ahead of idle Florida State in the US LBM coaches poll.

RK	TEAM	W-L	PVS
1.	Georgia	5-0	1
2.	Michigan	5-0	2
3.	Ohio State	4-0	3
4.	Texas	5-0	5
5.	Florida State	4-0	4

▶▶▶ In the AP media poll, the top seven remained the same: Georgia, Michigan, Texas, OSU, FSU, Penn State, Washington.

DYLAN WIDGER/USA TODAY SPORTS

To secure an acrobatic 29-yard touchdown catch, Roman Wilson pinned the ball against Isaac Gifford's helmet. "Man, that was God right there," J.J. McCarthy said, "and Roman Wilson."

THE PRIME NUMBER

22

Consecutive games lost by the Nebraska Cornhuskers to ranked opponents since 2016.

The Golden Gophers managed 10 first-half points, but that was it as the Wolverines quickly made it a laugher.

MATT KROHN/USA TODAY SPORTS

Proving once and for all he had recovered from knee surgery with a 36-yard pick-six, cornerback Will Johnson celebrated on the field with the football and then on the sideline with sunglasses. "I came off as late as I could," Johnson said. "Baited the quarterback into it."

Minny, ha ha

By Tony Garcia
THE BIG PICTURE

Two weeks earlier, Michigan coach Jim Harbaugh explained that there was a fine line between "Cool Guy Jim" and "Dead Serious Jim." Apparently, the line was crossed after a Will Johnson interception.

On the game's second play, Johnson intercepted a pass from Minnesota's Athan Kaliakmanis and took it back 36 yards for a pick-six.

The trophy piece wasn't as cool as, say, the Stanley Cup, but Michigan fans relished the chance to touch the Little Brown Jug, which pretty much had resided in Ann Arbor for a half-century.

Michigan made life miserable for Minnesota's leading receiver, Daniel Jackson, who later made All-Big Ten second team. Targeted seven times, he had two catches, though one was for a 35-yard TD.

As Johnson, a sophomore from Grosse Pointe South, ran back to the sideline to put on the Turnover Buffs sunglasses he introduced in 2022 and pose for pictures with his teammates, Harbaugh — who did his best not to get involved in antics during games — couldn't help but slide into the picture and smile.

"Just came over to congratulate Will, and they kind of threw me in," Harbaugh said with a laugh. "Can't start the game better. Love the pick-six. It was a (run-pass option), Will had good eyes, made the catch and finished it off."

Late in the third quarter, safety Keon Sabb scored on a 28-yard interception return. It was that kind of night for the Wolverines, who pummeled Minnesota from start to finish, 52-10.

Harbaugh congratulated Sabb with a love pat as he came off the field. Even with the score now 45-10, Harbaugh avoided the Buffs photo shoot.

"Two pick-sixes, have to go back to 2017 … against Cincinnati, remember that well," Harbaugh said. "So it was cool, very cool."

Quarterback J.J. McCarthy was surgical as he completed 14 of 20 passes for 219 yards and a touchdown and did plenty of damage on the ground, rushing four times for 17 yards and two touchdowns, lowering a shoulder on a five-yarder and using a stiff arm on a seven-yarder.

"Definitely mixed emotions," said left tackle LaDarius Henderson of watching McCarthy battle his way to the goal line. "You're always like, 'Ahh, don't do too much,' but then again you're like, 'Man, this guy's a dawg.'"

"Dawg, D-A-W-G," Harbaugh later called McCarthy. "Disciplined Athlete With Grit."

At least McCarthy got to sit out the fourth quarter for the fifth time in six games.

U-M needed Blake Corum to carry the ball only nine times; still, his 69 yards were a game-high and he scored on a one-yard run, his 10th touchdown of the season, still all five yards or fewer.

But the story was again the defense. Besides the pick-sixes, the Wolverines had seven tackles for loss, four pass breakups, four quarterback hurries and two sacks. They allowed only 169 yards — 117 on the ground and 52 through the air.

"It speaks for itself, right?" Harbaugh said of his defense. "We haven't had any points scored against us in the third quarter. … We just keep getting better and better on the defensive front."

Part of that was the return of tackle Mason Graham, who played with a giant club on his left arm because of hand surgery. He had a team-high six tackles, including two for a loss with a sack (after which he pretended to "row the boat" in celebration).

"I've been hungry to get back on the field with my guys," said Graham, a sophomore.

In four third-quarter possessions, Michigan held Minnesota to three three-and-outs and an interception. The Gophers ran eight times for seven yards.

In the first 20½ minutes of the second half, the Wolverines outscored the Gophers, 28-0, and outgained them, 212-7.

Harbaugh described the Wolverines' blowout in two words.

"Pretty dominant," he said. "Just about anybody you bring up, I'll say the same thing."

MATT KROHN/USA TODAY SPORTS

Although some fans, teammates and coaches might have covered their eyes fearing an injury, J.J. McCarthy lowered a shoulder, flew for the pylon and used a stiff arm to score two touchdowns. "Dawg, D-A-W-G," Jim Harbaugh called him. "Disciplined Athlete With Grit."

THE PREAMBLE

▶▶▶ Expected to contend in the Big Ten West, Minnesota sported only a 3-2 overall and 1-1 conference records. The Golden Gophers were 19½-point underdogs against Michigan in a primetime game because they needed 10 points in the final 2:32 to beat Nebraska, 13-10, and they blew a 21-point fourth-quarter lead in an overtime loss to Northwestern. Also, U-M had captured the Little Brown Jug, the oldest trophy in college football, 42 times in the last 46 meetings.

▶▶▶ Noted for the catchphrases "Row The Boat" and "Ski-U-Mah," Gophers coach P.J. Fleck took a shine to a September comment by Jim Harbaugh about the job of U-M's acting head coaches in his absence. "Be the guardian of victory," Harbaugh had said. "There's no offense. There's no defense. It's a we-defense." Fleck said at his weekly news conference: "Coach Harbaugh does a great job of promoting team, team, team, team. The 'we-fense.' And I love that. ... When you watch their team, they all talk about the team, they all play for the team."

MATT KROHN/USA TODAY SPORTS

In his second season at Michigan after transferring from Central Florida (and fifth year overall in college), defensive lineman Cam Goode proved to be an immovable object at 6-feet-1 and 314 pounds. On this night, he made four tackles.

MATT KROHN/USA TODAY SPORTS

Fifth-year senior Cornelius Johnson hauled in a 49-yard pass midway through the second quarter. From Greenwich, Connecticut, Johnson finished with three catches for 86 yards — all in the first half.

THE PLAY-BY-PLAY

▶▶▶ After Will Johnson's early pick-six, the teams traded first-quarter field goals. Then Blake Corum and J.J. McCarthy ran for touchdowns. But with six seconds left in the half, U-M's Mike Sainristil was beaten for a 35-yard touchdown. That made the Gophers the first team to reach double digits against the country's top-ranked scoring defense (6.0 points a game) and fourth-ranked total defense (246.2 yards).

▶▶▶ Minnesota had no additional highlights. In the third quarter, McCarthy scored again, he hit Colston Loveland for a 24-yard TD, and Keon Sabb recorded a 28-yard pick-six. In the fourth quarter, Jack Tuttle, apparently established as the No. 2 QB, led a 70-yard scoring drive that ended with a two-yard run by Leon Franklin, the first TD in his four years on the team.

▶▶▶ The Wolverines rushed for 191 yards on 33 carries (5.8 a pop), just missing their third straight 200-yard game.

THE PRIME NUMBER

22

Consecutive Big Ten victories by the Wolverines — including two conference championship games — and total victories as a starter by J.J. McCarthy — his only loss coming to TCU in the CFP semifinals.

THE PRESS BOX

▶▶▶ **CHIP SCOGGINS, MINNEAPOLIS STAR TRIBUNE:** "The Wolverines could have picked their margin of victory before kickoff. Truthfully, they could have left the Little Brown Jug at home because there was 0.0000000001 percent chance that trophy was changing hands."

▶▶▶ **SHAWN WINDSOR, DETROIT FREE PRESS:** "Nebraska and Minnesota may not be good football teams. But they are Big Ten football teams. And the Wolverines are making them look like they have no business in the Big Ten."

▶▶▶ **TONY GARCIA, DETROIT FREE PRESS:** "Michigan has the best defense in the country. It's because for the first time this season, Mason Graham and Will Johnson were on the field together working at full capacity."

MATT KROHN/USA TODAY SPORTS

Although his night ended in the third quarter, J.J. McCarthy led the sideline cheering when seldom-used Leon Franklin scored on a two-yard run in the fourth quarter.

THE PROCLAMATIONS

▶▶▶ **MINNESOTA COACH P.J. FLECK:** "They're as good as advertised. They're the best football team I've seen in 11 years as a head coach. We got beat tonight, period. In every facet."

▶▶▶ **COACH JIM HARBAUGH:** "There's a lot of great quarterbacks around the country. You know, play for play, J.J. McCarthy — maybe I'm a little biased, I'm trying not to be — but I think he's the best one. I really do. Certainly no one we'd rather have."

THE POLLS

▶▶▶ No. 12 Oklahoma's last-minute victory over No. 4 Texas, 34-30, shook up the US LBM coaches poll. Big movers: Washington from No. 8 to No. 6, Oklahoma to No. 7, Southern Cal from No. 7 to No. 9. Texas fell to 11th, right behind Alabama.

RK	TEAM	W-L	PVS
1.	Georgia	6-0	1
2.	Michigan	6-0	2
3.	Ohio State	5-0	3
4.	Florida State	5-0	5
5.	Penn State	5-0	6

▶▶▶ The top 10 in the AP media poll: Georgia, U-M, OSU, FSU, Oklahoma, Penn State, Washington, Oregon, Texas, USC.

The Wolverines were hardly on fire, but they still found it easy to extinguish the Hoosiers' competitive flame.

JUNFU HAN/DETROIT FREE PRESS

Aided by pressure from Josaiah Stewart, linebacker Michael Barrett (right) recorded a strip sack on Indiana's Tayven Jackson and recovered the fumble midway through the third quarter. "I was waiting for my turn to be a jolly good fellow," Barrett said. "So it feels great."

Stop, drop & roll

By Tony Garcia
THE BIG PICTURE

Michigan's start against Indiana was almost as sloppy as the weather on a wet, gray October afternoon in Ann Arbor.

The offensive line allowed a sack on each of the Wolverines' first two possessions, which led to consecutive three-and-outs. Two subsequent punts failed to pin the Hoosiers inside their 20. And although Michigan came away with an interception in its red zone after Indiana went as far as the U-M 10, the Hoosiers put together another lengthy drive on their next turn, which ended with a 44-yard trick play for a touchdown.

JUNFU HAN/DETROIT FREE PRESS

Two plays after Indiana took a 7-0 lead, linebacker Aaron Casey got a strip sack on J.J. McCarthy. But the fumble bounced out of bounds at the U-M 23. On third-and-10, McCarthy hit Colston Loveland for 13 yards, and eight plays later Blake Corum breached the end zone.

With 2:17 left in the first quarter, the second-ranked Wolverines trailed, 7-0, and had been outgained, 141 yards to minus-eight yards.

The game didn't stay that lopsided for long. Instead, it turned totally in Michigan's favor. The Wolverines scored 52 unanswered points — seven touchdowns and a field goal on their final eight possessions — to waltz to a 52-7 victory.

"Tremendous job responding," coach Jim Harbaugh said. "There's a devotion to the fundamentals of Michigan football, and you just go to work responding. That's the best strategy you can do."

Quarterback J.J. McCarthy, sensational again, made several highlight plays, including one late in the first half when he avoided the rush from his blind side, turned and ran left before a long shovel pass to Donovan Edwards for a gain of 16. Two plays later, Blake Corum scored for a 21-7 half-time lead.

On another such play, third-and-10 early in the second half, McCarthy scrambled right, appeared as if he was going to run for the first down, then at the last moment flipped the ball to Colston Loveland for a 54-yard touchdown reception for a 28-7 lead.

"I was able to escape the pocket, then it was two-on-one with that defender and me and Colston," McCarthy said. "I told (Loveland), go up field, so he's got to pick his poison, and he picked the wrong one."

McCarthy finished 14-for-17 passing for 222 yards and three touchdowns and added 27 rushing yards. Jack Tuttle came in as his replacement late in the third quarter against his former team and completed all five of his pass attempts for 22 yards and a four-yard touchdown pass to freshman Karmello English.

"The other thing that really hit me during this game, there's so many players to talk about," Harbaugh said. "So many great performances by every position group, by every player that was out there. And you see the development, you see the plays that they're making.

"Then the next wave of young guys, you see them coming up."

Michigan, though, struggled at times on the ground.

The running game took a hit when Kalel Mullings was ruled out with a hand injury. In all, the Wolverines ran 42 times for 163 yards, its lowest total since the opener and only for 3.9 yards a carry.

Corum led the way with 13 rushes for 52 yards and two touchdowns. Edwards ran nine times for 20 yards, although he scored his first TD of the season on a short fourth-quarter rush.

Harbaugh said it could be Edwards' "first olive."

"They're packed in so tight, the big screw top is wide (open), you unscrew it and you turn the olive jar over, nothing comes out because they're packed in so tight," Harbaugh said. "But if you can get just one to shake loose, they all start flopping out."

A freshman from West Bloomfield, Semaj Morgan scored his second TD of the season on a highlight-reel seven-yard screen pass.
JUNFU HAN/DETROIT FREE PRESS

THE PREAMBLE

▶▶▶ Since Indiana finished 6-2 in the pandemic-shortened 2020 season, which included its first victory over Michigan in 33 years, the Hoosiers had fallen on hard times. They owned a 2-18 Big Ten record since their 2021 opener. They were 2-3 overall and 0-2 Big Ten in 2023 and were averaging only 15.8 points a game against FBS opponents. During its just completed bye week, coach Tom Allen fired offensive coordinator Walt Bell. No wonder the Hoosiers were 33½-point underdogs coming to the Big House.

▶▶▶ Bell's replacement, Rod Carey, and Allen, under fire in Year 7, elected to rotate two quarterbacks and give them quicker reads on short routes. The strategy worked for a quarter and then failed spectacularly. The QBs didn't complete 50 percent of their passes (13 of 28), threw for only 96 yards, heaved two interceptions, lost two fumbles and were sacked four times.

THE PRIME NUMBER

19

Consecutive Big Ten victories by the Wolverines — including two conference championship games — matching the longest streak in program history (1990-92) and tying the fourth-longest streak in conference history.

THE PLAY-BY-PLAY

▶▶▶ Indiana's 141 yards in the first quarter were more than Michigan had allowed in a first half all season. But the Hoosiers managed only 40 yards on their next seven possessions.

▶▶▶ U-M's go-ahead touchdown came on a fourth-and-goal from Indiana's 2. McCarthy found Roman Wilson alone crossing the end zone for his ninth TD catch of the season, the most by a U-M receiver since Mario Manningham's 12 in 2007.

▶▶▶ Rod Moore and Keon Sabb each had an interception, Michael Barrett recorded a strip sack and recovered the fumble, and Jaylen Harrell forced another fumble that was recovered by Mason Graham.

▶▶▶ Two weeks earlier, Harbaugh decided his players should sing *For He's a Jolly Good Fellow* in the locker room to the game's top player. Serenaded this day were freshman receiver Semaj Morgan, who broke four tackles to score on a seven-yard screen pass, and Barrett, a sixth-year linebacker and a captain.

A junior edge rusher from Mansfield, Massachusetts, TJ Guy dragged down Indiana quarterback Brendan Sorsby late in the fourth quarter. On the Hoosiers' final drive, which covered 51 yards in 13 plays, Guy made three tackles before Indiana stalled at the U-M 31.

THE PRESS BOX

▶▶▶ **MATTHEW GLENESK, INDIANAPOLIS STAR:** "After the first quarter Saturday, it was Indiana 7, Michigan 0. No, really."

▶▶▶ **JEFF SEIDEL, DETROIT FREE PRESS:** "This Michigan team just sounded different. It talked differently. From 'scrambled eggs' pass plays. To 'olive jar' breakthrough moments. To 'master class' coaching. To 'jolly good fellow' celebrations. To the 'bully' mentality. This team was different. It had its own vocabulary. Its own way of doing things."

▶▶▶ **RAINER SABIN, DETROIT FREE PRESS:** "The Wolverines did their best to put on a show. Under light rain and a blanket of gray, J.J. McCarthy played with his usual flair, running and throwing while sometimes doing a little of each on the same play."

Although a tight end, Colston Loveland wasn't about to be caught by Louis Moore, an Indiana defensive back. Loveland's 54-yard TD reception put Michigan up, 28-7, early in the third quarter.

THE PROCLAMATIONS

▶▶▶ **LINEBACKER MICHAEL BARRETT:** "My favorite thing is watching their hope slowly go away, watching that fight just kind of diminish away from them. It kind of gets to the point where they are just like, 'Let's go home.' That's kind of my favorite feeling."

▶▶▶ **ATHLETIC DIRECTOR WARDE MANUEL:** "Hey, Jim, you missed one coach in your praise. Great job by you."

THE POLLS

▶▶▶ With a 36-33 victory over Oregon, which fell from No. 8 to No. 11, Washington jumped Penn State in the US LBM coaches poll. Eight Power Five teams remained unbeaten: the top five, No. 6 PSU, No. 7 Oklahoma and No. 10 North Carolina. With one loss, Texas and Alabama were tied at No. 8.

RK	TEAM	W-L	PVS
1.	Georgia	7-0	1
2.	Michigan	7-0	2
3.	Ohio State	6-0	3
4.	Florida State	6-0	4
5.	Washington	6-0	6

▶▶▶ The top 10 in the AP media poll: Georgia, U-M, OSU, FSU, Washington, Oklahoma, PSU, Texas, Oregon, North Carolina.

TOO HOT TO HANDLE

ADAM CAIRNS/USA TODAY SPORTS

Michigan coach Jim Harbaugh, with his headset, and off-the-field analyst Connor Stalions, with his papers, had their eyes glued to the field as the Wolverines battled the Buckeyes in November 2022 at Ohio Stadium. Michigan won that clash of unbeatens, 45-23.

In less a year, the rivalry between U-M and MSU was flipped on its head, thanks to some unsanctioned affairs.

By Gene Myers

By the time U-M/MSU rivalry week rolled around in mid-October, the Spartans were in disarray — haunted by past, present and future demons — and the Wolverines were a team of destiny — boasting a sledgehammer of a defense (first in fewest points allowed, second in fewest yards allowed) and a steamroller of an offense (beating its Big Ten rivals by progressively greater margins, Rutgers by 24, Nebraska by 38, Minnesota by 42, Indiana by 45).

The pushing, shoving and jawing on the field after Michigan's 29-7 victory over Michigan State in October 2022 was but a prelude to the violence about to erupt in the Lloyd Carr Tunnel at Michigan Stadium. Eventually, seven Spartans faced criminal charges.

But three days before kick-off — the first of the rivalry's 116 meetings to start under the lights at Spartan Stadium — Michigan State out of the blue had company in the Big Ten misery index. The NCAA informed Michigan that a new investigation had started to determine whether the Wolverines used in-person scouting to steal opponents' signs, a practice outlawed for nearly three decades.

THE BACKSTORY, PART I

The U-M/MSU clash came 358 days after a notorious

postgame tunnel fight at Michigan Stadium between two Wolverines and numerous Spartans that resulted in eight MSU players being suspended, seven of whom faced criminal charges, and a black eye on the series.

Two Wolverines — cornerbacks Gemon Green, a starting fifth-year senior, and Ja'Den McBurrows, a redshirt freshman who wore No. 1 but had yet to play that season — walked and skipped into the MSU entourage after U-M's 29-7 victory. Each carried his helmet. They were attacked by numerous Spartans.

McBurrows was tossed

against metal doors. Defensive end Itayvion (Tank) Brown picked him up and threw him back through the doors, upon which defensive end Zion Young and defensive back Angelo Grose landed punches and shoved him to the ground. Young kicked at McBurrows as he popped up and spun away from the pile toward his locker room side of the tunnel. MSU's Khary Crump swung — and struck — Green with his white helmet.

Six Spartans were charged with assault-related misdemeanors. Crump, a redshirt sophomore defensive back,

faced a charge of felonious assault with a deadly weapon, which carried a maximum sentence of four years in prison.

In January 2023, Crump pled down to misdemeanor counts of assault/battery and disorderly conduct person-jostling and avoided jail time. He received early discharge from his 12-month probation in August, had all charges wiped from his record through the Holmes Youthful Trainee Act, missed the first eight games of the season because of a Big Ten suspension and made the Big Ten's all-academic team. The

other Spartans enrolled in a court-supervised diversionary program to dismiss their charges in exchange for community service and good behavior.

A month after the tunnel assaults, Big Ten commissioner Kevin Warren levied a $100,000 fine against MSU, the largest in conference history, surpassing the $40,000 fine assessed to U-M basketball coach Juwan Howard for

ROBERT GODDIN/USA TODAY SPORTS
Commissioner Kevin Warren determined MSU and U-M "did not represent the level of sportsmanship that is expected from the Big Ten conference and its member institutions."

hitting a Wisconsin assistant in February 2022. Warren's son, Powers, was a seldom-used sixth-year tight end for MSU.

Michigan was reprimanded for failing "to provide adequate protection for personnel of both home and visiting teams when entering and leaving playing arenas." U-M previously had been privately reprimanded by the Big Ten; other tunnel incidents occurred against Ohio State in 2021 and Penn State in 2022.

In January 2023, U-M announced it would remove 45 seats to widen access to and from the tunnel.

THE BACKSTORY, PART II

Mel Tucker's fourth season as MSU's coach lasted only two games. He was suspended Sept. 11 and fired on Sept. 27 for not conducting himself "professionally and ethically, with integrity and sportsmanship at all times," according to his termination letter.

His life unraveled hours after the Spartans raised their record to 2-0 with an uninspiring blowout of Richmond. A *USA TODAY* investigation revealed that two years after Tucker — one of the country's highest-paid coaches — and Brenda Tracy — a prominent rape survivor — teamed up to fight sexual violence in

sports, the activist accused the coach of the same misconduct they spoke out against.

USA TODAY's Kenny Jacoby reported that over eight months, Tucker and Tracy developed a professional relationship centered on her advocacy work with her nonprofit, Set The Expectation. He invited her to MSU three times — twice to talk with his players and staff and once to be an honorary captain at the spring game. She was paid $10,000 for her first visit in August 2021.

But on April 28, 2022, a phone call changed everything. According to a complaint Tracy filed in December 2022 with MSU's Title IX office, Tucker made sexual comments about her and masturbated during the call. She said that triggered wounds from her 1998 gang rape by four football players

Mark Dantonio mingled with AD Alan Haller before MSU's opener. Two weeks later, Dantonio was on the field with the coaching staff.
NICK KING/LANSING STATE JOURNAL

at Oregon State.

Tucker told a Title IX investigator that he had masturbated but characterized the call as consensual phone sex. The Title IX inquiry remained open with a hearing scheduled for MSU's bye week in early October.

In a statement from his lawyer, Tucker called Tracy's allegations "completely false," said they had a "personal relationship" and accused MSU of using the investigation to avoid paying off his hefty contract.

On Sept. 18, MSU athletic director Alan Haller sent Tucker a letter saying that he would be terminated for cause. MSU did not need to wait for the Title IX hearing, Haller wrote, because Tucker admitted to behavior in clear violation of his contract.

"It is decidedly unprofessional and unethical to flirt, make sexual comments, and masturbate while on the phone with a university vendor," Haller wrote. "The unprofessional and unethical behavior is particularly egregious given that the vendor at issue was contract-

ed by the university for the sole purpose of educating student-athletes on, and preventing instances of, inappropriate sexual misconduct."

The letter also said Tucker had "brought public disrespect, contempt and ridicule upon the university."

Tucker elected to skip the Title IX hearing. On Oct. 25, in a 73-page report, a university hearing officer determined Tucker sexually harassed and exploited Tracy during their April 2022 phone call, made unwanted sexual advances in the months before the call and engaged in quid pro quo sexual harassment after the call by ending their business relationship.

"My first reaction was tears of relief," Tracy told *USA TODAY*.

At issue remained the roughly $80 million left on a 10-year, $95 million contract Tucker signed in November 2021 while the Spartans were en route to an 11-2 record and a top-10 finish. As the calendar flipped to 2024, no signs of money changing hands or of lawsuits being filed were apparent. Tucker exited with

a 20-14 record (.588) but only a 10-9 record (6-9 against Power Five schools) since upsetting Michigan in 2021.

Already a suspect team when Tucker was suspended, the Spartans lost their next four games — two were blowouts, two were close — with assistant Harlon Barnett as interim head coach. Haller convinced Mark Dantonio, at 67, to come out of retirement as an associate head coach to advise Barnett.

Barnett, 56, was a three-year starting defensive back in the late 1980s, including on the Rose Bowl winners in the 1987 season. He spent 14 of his previous 20 seasons in college coaching at his alma mater, the last three as Tucker's secondary coach and 11 as an assistant for Dantonio.

THE NCAA'S CROSSHAIRS

On Thursday before the rivalry game, the hot topic turned from turmoil in the tunnel, the Spartans' next coach and the Wolverines' national title hopes to bombshell news that the NCAA had

launched another investigation of Michigan's program.

Yahoo! Sports broke the story and also reported that two of U-M's opponents became aware U-M knew their play signals. The Big Ten released a statement that the conference and U-M were notified of the investigation late Wednesday and that the conference had notified MSU and future opponents.

Sign stealing wasn't illegal in college football; to the contrary, it was a timeless and colorful practice for teams to try to decipher their rivals' signals.

But in 1994, the NCAA outlawed in-person scouting of opponents, largely as a cost-saving measure. According to NCAA bylaw 11.6.1: "Off-campus, in-person scouting of future opponents (in the same season) is prohibited." However, teams generally were provided extensive video footage of their opponents, which in turn could be used to scout tendencies and decode signals.

The NCAA football rule book also stated that "any attempt to record, either through audio or video means, any signals given by an opposing player, coach or other team personnel is prohibited" (though with exceptions).

No specific penalties were listed for such violations.

In separate statements, Harbaugh and athletic director Warde Manuel pledged cooperation with the NCAA investigation, and Harbaugh denied participating in a sign-stealing scheme.

"I do not have any knowledge or information regarding the University of Michigan football program illegally stealing signals, nor have I

directed any staff member or others to participate in an off-campus scouting assignment," he said. "I have no awareness of anyone on our staff having done that or having directed that action.

"I do not condone or tolerate anyone doing anything illegal or against NCAA rules. No matter what program or organization that I have led throughout my career, my instructions and awareness of how we scout opponents have always been firmly within the rules."

Effective for 2023, the NCAA strengthened bylaw 11.1.1.1 to put the onus for all violations on the head coach, an effort to stop coaches from turning a blind eye to infractions to maintain deniability. The bylaw read: "An institution's head coach shall be responsible for the head coach's actions and the actions of all institutional staff members who report, directly or indirectly, to the head coach."

Thursday's developments turned out to be a drip. Friday, the faucet was turned on full force. A new revelation, allegation or hot take seemed to pop up every few days for the rest of the season. Allegations of cheating by one of the sport's iconic schools piqued a frenzy across the country — even though every pundit and fan knew every team, in one way or another, sought to swipe its rivals' signals.

On Friday morning, college football was introduced to a low-level U-M staffer named Connor Stalions. By Friday afternoon, Michigan had suspended Stalions — with pay.

ESPN.com identified Stalions, a 28-year-old off-the-field analyst with a military background, as "a person of interest" in the NCAA's investigation into whether Michigan stole signs with in-person scouting. Citing a variety of unnamed sources in its report, including ones with U-M and Big Ten ties, ESPN also said that the NCAA's enforcement staff sought immediate access to Stalions' computer and that U-M had used an "elaborate" scouting system to swipe signals from future opponents since at least 2021.

No details about how the system operated were provided. However, ESPN said coaches and administrators around the Big Ten were rattled by the allegations and feared it involved the use of recording devices.

"This is worse than both the Astros and the Patriots," ESPN quoted a conference source as saying. "It's both use of technology for a competitive advantage, and there's allegations that they are filming prior games, not just in-game. If it was just an in-game situation, that's different. Going and filming somewhere you're not supposed to be, it's illegal. It's too much of an advantage."

Yahoo! Sports soon after reported that other Big Ten football staffs knew of Stalions and his sign-stealing expertise well before the NCAA got involved. An unidentified head coach told the website: "We were told to be careful because they had a guy who could pick plays. It was too late in the week to change our signals, but another staff did tell us about (Stalions)." And another conference coach went further: "I once told him, 'We know what kind of (expletive) you are doing and it's (expletive) up."

Manuel announced that Stalions had been suspended with pay until the conclusion of the NCAA investigation.

NICK KING/LANSING STATE JOURNAL

What good was a rivalry if you couldn't poke fun at your foe, right? Two Michigan State fans trolled Jim Harbaugh before the Wolverines dismantled MSU, 49-0, at Spartan Stadium.

In the next week, news report after news report painted a picture of how Stalions allegedly tried to master the signals for opposing teams. But on this day, the rush was to figure out who heck this guy was and how a superfan from Lake Orion, Michigan, rose to be a full-time staffer whose Instagram account included photos on the sideline next to former defensive coordinators Don Brown and Mike Macdonald.

After ESPN's report, Stalions' social media accounts were deleted or deactivated. Pieced together was that Stalions graduated from Lake Orion High in 2013 and the U.S. Naval Academy in 2017. He was stationed at Camp Pendleton in Southern California as a captain in the Marines. He left the military after his five-year commitment and was hired as an analyst by U-M in May 2022, at an annual salary of $55,000.

ESPN reported that although Stalions technically worked in the recruiting department, it was well-known around Schembechler Hall that he spent his time decoding opponents' signals, often watching television copies of games. "He had one role," according to a source with knowledge of U-M's staff.

On his LinkedIn profile, Stalions wrote that he tried to "employ Marine Corps philosophies and tactics into the sport of football regarding strategies in staffing, recruiting, scouting, intelligence, planning and more." He listed among his skills "identifying the opponent's most likely course of action and most dangerous course of action" and "identifying and exploiting critical vulnerabilities and centers of gravity in the opponent scouting process."

Also on LinkedIn, he said he had been a volunteer assistant since May 2015, apparently at first working at camps and clinics during his summers and then "flying back (and) forth on my own dime, assisting the defensive staff."

Later profiles, by news organizations local and national, fleshed out Stalions' rise from obscurity to notoriety. All portrayed him as driven, ambitious, analytical and intelligent. All underscored that from an early age he wanted to be associated with Michigan football, as the head coach in the best of possible worlds.

"I've grown up my entire life with a vision to coach football at Michigan," Stalions told the nonprofit Soldiers to Sidelines after being selected its coach of the month for January 2022. "I stopped playing football junior year of high school to coach with my dad's eighth-grade football team."

His parents were U-M graduates, season-ticket holders, thrilled when Brady Hoke was fired and Harbaugh hired, and each honored as a teacher-of-the-year at Scripps Middle School in Lake Orion, located about a half-hour from Detroit.

In high school, Stalions won numerous awards, served as a class officer, was a National Honor Society member and played basketball. Although accepted by U-M, Stalions elected to attend Navy. He told Soldiers to Sidelines that because most Power Five coaches were collegiate players and he lacked that talent, he needed a different path to his dream career. He said he realized numerous notable coaches — Bo Schembechler, Woody Hayes, John Wooden, Vince Lombardi, Nick Saban and Bill Belichick — served in the military or had strong ties to a military academy.

At Navy, Stalions volunteered with the football program, spending one year in the video department and three in recruiting. He also worked to ingratiate himself with Michigan's staff. Once stationed in Southern California, according to the *Detroit News*, Stalions purchased a five-bedroom, three-bathroom home for $465,000, which he told Soldiers to Sidelines he rented through Airbnb to finance his trips to Ann Arbor. At times, he said, he slept on his couch or in his car.

Sports Illustrated reviewed texts from early 2021 between Stalions and an unnamed student at a Power Five school aiming for a career in college football. Stalions boasted: "I'm close to the whole staff" and "pre-COVID, stole opponent signals during the week watching TV copies then flew to the game and stood next to Gattis and told him what coverage/pressure he was gettin'." (Josh Gattis was the offensive coordinator at the time.)

Stalions texted that he had a Google document 550 to 600 pages long that he curated daily and called the Michigan Manifesto. It was supposedly a long-range plan to run the U-M program, crafted with two low-level staffers at other college programs. "Any idea you could ever have," he texted, "there's a place where it belongs in the document. It's super organized."

State of rivalry? Not in East Lansing, where the Wolverines smashed the Spartans in nearly every way imaginable.

KIRTHMON F. DOZIER/DETROIT FREE PRESS

J.J. McCarthy and his teammates hoisted the Paul Bunyan Trophy for the second straight season. In the third quarter, Mike Sainristil swiped an MSU pass and dashed 72 yards for a pick-six. In the end zone, Sainristil struck the same pose as the trophy.

Paul & chain

By Mitch Albom
THE BIG PICTURE

I t felt less like a football game than a fraternity prank, where the upperclassmen leave the pledges in their underwear, in the cold, in the middle of a corn field. It was 28-0 at halftime, 42-0 after three quarters, and backups-to-the-backups making it 49-0 just before the final gun.

Somewhere in this mass of humanity the Wolverines were exerting their will upon the Spartans. Michigan State managed only 182 yards — 133 through the air and 49 on the ground. KIRTHMON F. DOZIER/DFP

Whatever was left of Michigan State's sinking balloon of a season was in tatters, torn and shredded. Saturday night's shellacking at the hands of Michigan was the ugly bookend to A Year of Living Terribly, starting with last October's drubbing in Ann Arbor, followed by the infamous tunnel fight in the Big House, then a 5-7 season record, no bowl, and last month Mel Tucker's firing after a sexual harassment scandal.

Talk about a funk. The Spartans, now 2-5, have lost every game since Tucker left the sidelines, and while faithful fans already had written off this season with an asterisk, there was a small, silent hope that if the Spartans could upset the Wolverines, knock those arrogant Ann Arborites off their lofty No. 2-in-the-country pedestal, then salvation could yet be found in 2023.

Keep looking. This was

never a game. Never a contest. It was an exhibition. It was Michigan as Picasso, painting Spartan Stadium in maize and blue, then wiping its brushes with the MSU uniforms.

Forty-nine points and nearly 500 yards on offense? Zero points allowed and two turnovers on defense?

"I thought we were really good," coach Jim Harbaugh told NBC after this game ended. "Our guys played really hard."

And when he said "our guys," he meant all of them. Subs played. Subs-to-the-subs played. By the end, I thought the U-M trainers and bus drivers were out there.

And then, when it was over, there was this: Michigan nickelback Mike Sainristil, who had a whale of a game, including a 72-yard interception return for a touchdown, was doing an NBC interview when he stopped to wave over backup Ja'Den McBurrows.

"Come here! Come here! Real quick!" he yelled, pulling in the teammate who at the end of last year's contest was thrown to floor, dragged, hit and kicked by several Spartans in the Big House tunnel, an incident that muddied this rivalry in a big way.

"The adversity he went through with what happened last year in that tunnel," Sainristil hollered, "to come out and have a game like he did tonight — an interception, three or four tackles. Ja'Den McBurrows, stay tuned!"

They ran off together, as happy as a pair of lottery winners. McBurrows did get a measure of retribution, his first career interception, even if it did come late in a game that had long since been decided.

Michigan fans who had ventured to East Lansing witnessed it. By that point, many Spartans fans already had left the stadium.

Given what took place, you could hardly blame them. Because this was MSU's worst home loss in the 100-year history of Spartan Stadium.

Look. Michigan had elite talent. The Spartans had been reeling under all that has happened. The cobbled lead-

Coach Jim Harbaugh offered congratulations to tailback Donovan Edwards, tight end Colston Loveland and center Drake Nugent after a touchdown. Harbaugh raised his record against MSU to 5-4. "A buzzsaw," he said. "Most complete game of the season."

ership of Harlon Barnett as interim coach, Mark Dantonio as some kind of adviser, and athletic director Alan Haller combing the weeds for a potential new leader, wasn't exactly what we call "stability" for MSU players.

Still, this was their biggest game of the year. There had been previous seasons when the talent disparity favored Michigan. But the grit, the passion, the jealousies and the venom of this rivalry usually lifted players, sometimes beyond expectations. The hits were harder. The tackles were meaner. Weird things happened. Upsets took place.

Not on the first night game in the rivalry at Spartan Stadium. From the very start, the Spartans played as if they didn't think they belonged. They let the Wolverines march 84 yards on the opening drive, surrendering a long pass on a third-and-14 and giving up a touchdown run to Blake Corum on a third-and-goal.

MSU's Harlon Barnett only could shake his head: "Penalties and turnovers and not getting off the field on third down are things that, you can't win football games if you're doing those things."

MSU went for 26 yards on its first drive, followed by minus-five yards on its second drive, then six yards, three yards and six yards on its

remaining possessions of the first half. The punter had to be exhausted. You knew this was over long before halftime.

U-M quarterback J.J. McCarthy had such an easy time slicing through the MSU defense, you almost wanted to blindfold him to make it a fair fight. His accuracy was on full display, whipping touchdowns to his tight ends (three) and wide receivers (one) by splitting defenders or whizzing the ball past their ears. He finished with 287 passing yards, going 21-for-27, and spent half the night only breaking a sweat by cheering on the backups.

"We're always gonna keep pushing, we're always gonna keep wanting more," McCarthy told NBC, "whether it's the 1s is in there, 2s or 3s, we're always gonna keep pushing."

By the end, it might have been the 4s and 5s.

Michigan's defense continues to be the bloody card it leaves on the barroom table before departing. Already

setting records for allowing fewer than 10 points a game in its first seven contests, the U-M defenders threw a shutout, the first in the series at East Lansing since a 31-0 U-M victory in 1985. They had nine tackles for loss and three sacks, in addition to picks by Sainristil and McBurrows.

Michigan outscored MSU by a combined score of 78-7 the last two meetings. U-M outgained MSU in this meeting, 477-182. And next year they will play in Ann Arbor.

Meanwhile, MSU ended the awful night with an unexpected dose of gruesome, having to issue an apology for an image of Adolf Hitler that flashed on the giant scoreboard about 80 minutes before the game. The image was part of a trivia game that MSU said it contracted from a "third party" vendor.

"MSU will not be using the third-party source going forward," a school spokesman said in a statement.

What an ugly green mess.

Two days after another brilliant outing, J.J. McCarthy revealed: "I just stay focused and keep my life simple. Keeping to my meditation, keeping to being in this building, being around the guys."
KIRTHMON F. DOZIER/DFP

THE PREAMBLE

▶▶▶ For the first time in the 116 meetings of their bitter rivalry, the Wolverines and Spartans were to kick off in the nighttime at Spartan Stadium. At 2-4, the Spartans were 19½-point underdogs and losers four straight after the firing of Mel Tucker because of a sexual harassment scandal. The interim reins went to a long-time MSU favorite, Harlon Barnett, who won a Rose Bowl as an MSU defensive back and owned a 10-4 record against U-M as an assistant coach under Mark Dantonio and Tucker. Barnett vs. Jim Harbaugh marked the first time in the rivalry that alums for each team led their alma maters. "It's the best rivalry in football," Barnett said.

▶▶▶ Michigan's 29-7 victory in 2022 at the Big House ended with numerous Spartans pummeling defensive backs Gemon Green and Ja'Den McBurrows in the tunnel to the locker rooms. Green moved onto the pros, and McBurrows was a reserve who battled various injuries. Three of seven Spartans criminally charged in the incident were on the active roster: Angelo Grose, Brandon Wright and Zion Young, all starters on defense.

▶▶▶ In U-M's 37-33 loss in 2021 at Spartan Stadium, J.J. McCarthy, who played occasional series as a true freshman, lost a fumble late in the fourth quarter, which led to MSU's game-winning score. He admitted after the 2023 game that "the outcome of that game was definitely on my mind."

THE PLAY-BY-PLAY

▶▶▶ Michigan asserted its will immediately with a 12-play, 84-yard drive that took 6:05 and ended with a one-yard touchdown run by Blake Corum. Then the U-M defense stuffed MSU on a fourth-and-two near midfield. Five plays later, McCarthy scrambled out of trouble and on the run hit Roman Wilson for a 25-yard TD with 2:52 left in the first quarter.

▶▶▶ McCarthy threw two more TD passes in the second quarter, each 22 yards to tight end Colston Loveland. U-M's 28-0 halftime lead was the largest in the series at the half since U-M led by the same score in 1947, an eventual 55-0 victory.

▶▶▶ On the first drive of the second half, nickelback Mike Sainristil returned an interception 72 yards for his second pick-six of the season. He struck the same pose as the Paul Bunyan Trophy — just as he had done in 2021 when he caught a TD pass back in his days as a wide receiver. On U-M's first series of the third quarter, McCarthy threw an 11-yard TD pass to tight end AJ Barner for a 42-0 lead.

▶▶▶ For all the stellar stats and rankings for the U-M defense, it still lacked a shutout in 2023. McBurrows helped ensure U-M would have its first since a 59-0 wipeout of Connecticut in September 2022 and first in the rivalry since a 14-0 victory in 2000. McBurrows, a redshirt

KIRTHMON F. DOZIER/DETROIT FREE PRESS
Mike Sainristil and Ja'Den McBurrows — each with an interception — celebrated on the field. "It looked like he wanted to cry tears of joy," Sainristil said, "but he held it in."

sophomore, turned a deflected pass into his first career interception with 3:10 left in the game. The final points came on the final play: QB4 Alex Orji scored on a six-yard run and James Turner kicked his seventh extra point.

Once again his work long finished, J.J. McCarthy spent much of the second half rooting on his teammates, including a touchdown in the closing seconds.

THE PROCLAMATIONS

▶▶▶ **QUARTERBACK J.J. MCCARTHY:** "We do a tremendous job of keeping the main thing, the main thing, stay in the present moment, control what we can control and just strive to get better."

▶▶▶ **TAILBACK BLAKE CORUM ON MCCARTHY**: "He's a heck of a player. Where he was last year to this year, I'm proud of him, but I expect nothing less, just because the type of person he is. The work that I see him put in, the film I see him watch, he's amazing, man. So when it comes to the Heisman, I say put him up there. He deserves it."

▶▶▶ **COACH JIM HARBAUGH ON MCCARTHY:** "He's just so dangerous when he's out of the pocket, keeps his eyes down field and just hits the open receiver or runs it himself. ... He is a double-edged sword, can beat you in so many ways."

Besides his four touchdown passes, J.J. McCarthy broke off a 16-yard run. "The fame, the notoriety and all that," he said, "that's just a byproduct of the work we put in as a team."

THE PRIME NUMBER

3

Snaps taken by J.J. McCarthy in the second half after completing 20 of 26 passes for 276 yards and three touchdowns in the first half. His lone series in the third quarter ended with an 11-yard TD pass to AJ Barner.

Blake Corum opened the scoring with a one-yard run with 8:50 left in the first quarter. He didn't have a heavy workload, but his 59 rushing yards gave him 3,097 for his career, pushing him past Billy Taylor (3,072) for ninth most at U-M. Up next: Rob Lytle at 3,317.
KIRTHMON F. DOZIER/DFP

KIRTHMON F. DOZIER/DFP

About all Spartan Nation could do was root for the clock.

THE POLLS

▶▶▶ Two more unbeatens bit the dust: Penn State, which slipped from sixth to 10th in the US LBM coaches poll after a 20-12 loss to Ohio State, and North Carolina, which fell from 10th to 17th after losing, 31-27, to one-win Virginia. Six Power Five unbeatens remained: the top five in the poll and No. 6 Oklahoma.

RK	TEAM	W-L	PVS
1.	Georgia	8-0	1
2.	Michigan	8-0	2
3.	Ohio State	7-0	3
4.	Florida State	7-0	4
5.	Washington	7-0	5

▶▶▶ The top 10 in the AP media poll: Georgia, U-M, OSU, FSU, Washington, Oklahoma, Texas, Oregon, Alabama, PSU.

THE PRESS BOX

▶▶▶ **GRAHAM COUCH, LANSING STATE JOURNAL:** "Near the end of Harlon Barnett's news conference — 13 minutes of introspection and explanation and a few laughs through the pain — MSU's interim coach delivered a warning to the Wolverines that would make his mentor, Mark Dantonio, proud. Barnett had been asked whether he seriously considered not playing the game because of the alleged sign-stealing scheme. After shaking off the notion, he fired this barb Michigan's way: 'It don't get ya until it gets ya. Just remember that.'"

▶▶▶ **RAINER SABIN, DETROIT FREE PRESS:** "The Wolverines, Jim Harbaugh later said, were 'a real buzzsaw.' They tore through MSU, disassembling their in-state foe piece by piece with ruthless efficiency. It was cold-blooded, merciless, even a little bit mean. It was also full of intent. After the Wolverines went up by four touchdowns before halftime, Harbaugh entered a boisterous locker room and shared a few words. 'Leave no doubt,' he told them."

▶▶▶ **TONY GARCIA, DETROIT FREE PRESS:** "Entering the game with the cloud of another NCAA investigation hovering over the coaching staff, the Wolverines put the noise aside and came out and handled business in dominating fashion."

(STOLEN) SIGNS OF THE TIMES

BARBARA J. PERENIC/USA TODAY SPORTS

As the autumn trees changed colors, Michigan vs. Everyone seemed more like Big Ten vs. Michigan. The presidents were irked, the athletic directors were irked, the football coaches were irked. And you never could trust any of the mascots.

Even the mascots had jokes, but the sign-stealing scandal, ever expanding, was no laughing matter for the Wolverines.

By Gene Myers

When Michigan took the field for its next game, the Wolverines were trolled by a mascot. Purdue Pete donned a robe adorned with Ohio State logos while holding a cardboard replica of a recording device. Good ol' Pete aimed it at the Michigan sideline during the first half at the Big House.

After a bye week in the schedule and two weeks of accusatory headlines, Jim Harbaugh watched his second-ranked Wolverines warm up for a night game against lowly Purdue at the Big House. KIRTHMON F. DOZIER/DETROIT FREE PRESS

Purdue Pete was far from the only figure in the Big Ten who wanted a pound of flesh from the Wolverines. Instead of an under-the-radar bye week after its annihilation of Michigan State, Michigan faced awkward revelation after awkward revelation about the sign-stealing investigation. In the days before the Purdue game, the league's coaches and athletic directors in separate video calls with new commissioner Tony Petitti demanded immediate punishment for the Wolverines.

MSU's athletic director, Alan Haller, reportedly accused the league of hypocrisy because Petitti's predecessor, Kevin Warren, swiftly suspended eight Spartans after the 2022 tunnel incident, not waiting for the Big Ten — or legal authorities — to finish their investigations. At that time, U-M coach Jim Harbaugh pushed the hardest for punishment on all fronts: "It's clear what transpired. It seems very open and shut, as they say."

On Oct. 23, two days after the MSU game, ESPN reported that off-the-field analyst Connor Stalions purchased tickets with his personal cred-

it card to more than 30 games at 11 Big Ten schools over the last three years. At a cost of thousands of dollars from on-line brokers such as StubHub, the tickets were distributed electronically to at least three people around the country. Schools confirmed to ESPN the tickets were used.

Just as damaging, ESPN reported that the NCAA was expected to receive evidence from a Big Ten school in which its in-stadium surveillance video showed a person in a seat purchased by Stalions holding up his smartphone and appearing to film the home team's sideline the entire game.

Stalions also had purchased tickets on each sideline for the past weekend's game between Ohio State and Penn State. No one sat in the seats the day after he was revealed to be a person of interest in the NCAA investigation.

NCAA rules prohibited in-person scouting of opponents and the use of technology to record "any signals" used by opponents.

On Oct. 24, ESPN and Yahoo! Sports reported that Stalions purchased tickets to the 2021 and 2022 SEC

championship games, each of which featured eventual national champ Georgia. ESPN said a 12th Big Ten school confirmed that Stalions bought tickets to its games. And Yahoo said Stalions bought tickets for Tennessee-Kentucky in October 2022 and Oregon-Washington in November 2022.

On Oct. 25, the *Washington Post* reported that the NCAA's investigation started after an outside investigative firm approached the NCAA a week earlier with documents and videos the firm had obtained from computer drives maintained and accessed by multiple U-M coaches. The *Post*'s sources would not reveal who hired the outside firm, and while its report suggested that Stalions did not act alone, it pointed out that no evidence from the firm directly linked Harbaugh to the scheme.

The *Post* wrote: "Among the pieces of evidence presented ... was a detailed schedule of Michigan's planned sign-stealing travel for the rest of the season, listing opponents' schedules, which games Michigan scouts would attend and how much money was budgeted for travel and

tickets to scout each team."

The operation budgeted $15,000 to scout more than 40 games played by 10 opponents, according to the *Post*'s sources. The firm presented photographs to the NCAA of people it suspected were scouts for U-M aiming their smartphones at the sidelines, and it told the NCAA that videos from these games were uploaded to a computer drive accessed by Stalions and other staffers.

On Oct. 26, ESPN revealed that the NCAA's enforcement staff was on the U-M campus as part of its investigation. The *Free Press* reported that although the FBI was involved in the case, U-M police said the investigation of former co-offensive coordinator Matt Weiss for computer access crimes was not "related to the sign-stealing allegation in any way." Several news outlets, including the *Free Press*, reported that Harbaugh's never-ending contract talks were put on hold.

Also on Oct. 26, Yahoo reported that Texas Christian was aware of U-M's sign-stealing attempts heading into the 2022 College Football Playoff. In turn, the Horned Frogs crafted "dummy

Hired in April 2023 as the Big Ten's seventh commish, Tony Petitti faced a challenging summer when the Pac-12 imploded. The league already had a logistics nightmare preparing for USC and UCLA in 2024. The solution? Add Washington and Oregon! By fall, Petitti faced intraconference squabbling about a sign-stealing scandal.
ROBERT GODDIN/ USA TODAY SPORTS

signals" and used the Wolverines' supposed knowledge to trick them repeatedly. Several Big Ten teams reached out to TCU, including Ohio State, according to Yahoo. An unnamed coach called U-M's operation "the most elaborate signal stealing in the history of the world." A few weeks later, TCU coach Sonny Dykes confirmed Yahoo's account. "There's no secrets and honor among thieves and coaches," Dykes said. "So, you know, you start calling around and say, 'Tell us about Michigan,' and a lot of things come up. And so we had some time to sit and decide how we were going to handle this."

On Oct. 27, ESPN uncovered a former Division III player and coach who said he was paid a few hundred dollars and given a ticket to a U-M home game by Stalions

to scout games. The man did not want his name published because of privacy concerns.

He said he attended games at Rutgers and Penn State in 2022 and at Penn State in 2023. (And he did not attend the next day's Indiana-Penn State game in which Stalions sent him tickets.) The man apparently uploaded videos from his cellphone to a shared iPhone photo album.

"I didn't like it, but it's a gray line," the man told ESPN. "You can call me naïve, but no one is reading the bylaws."

On Oct. 29, *Sports Illustrated*'s Pat Forde reported that several sources at a Big Ten school said they were warned by another coach that U-M's ball boys on the opposing sideline would listen to play calls and relay the information across the field. They allegedly did so by holding a

football in one hand for a pass and the other for a run. However, the unnamed sources said they noticed no such behavior during their game against U-M.

On Oct. 30, Harbaugh used his weekly news conference to dispute a *Wall Street Journal* report that U-M had rescinded an offer to extend his contract.

On Oct. 31, the College Football Playoff committee revealed its initial rankings. Although Michigan was No. 2 in the coaches and media polls, the committee, which included U-M athletic director Warde Manuel, pegged the Wolverines at No. 3, behind Ohio State and Georgia. Florida State was No. 4. U-M's lackluster schedule certainly did not help its case for a higher ranking.

But U-M received good

news from the committee chair, Boo Corrigan, North Carolina State's AD. Asked during ESPN's reveal show by host Rece Davis about the developing sign-stealing allegations, Corrigan replied: "Our job, as we look at it, is to rank the teams, to follow the protocols. And as we went through it, that really wasn't part of any of the discussions that occurred during our time together. It's an NCAA issue, it's not a CFP issue."

The CFP's executive director, Bill Hancock, later told reporters: "You have to remember that these are allegations at this point and not facts."

Also on Oct. 31, Central Michigan revealed it was trying to determine whether Stalions was on the Chippewas' sideline during their Sept. 1 season opener at Michigan State. Photos of a

Internet sleuths noticed a man who looked like Connor Stalions on Central Michigan's sideline for its opener at Michigan State. CMU said it would investigate, and the NCAA got involved, too.

man wearing CMU gear and sunglasses and carrying a clipboard with a striking resemblance to Stalions started appearing on the internet the previous evening.

Later that Halloween evening, after CMU beat Northern Illinois, 37-31, at Mount Pleasant, coach Jim McElwain addressed the issue without being asked. "Before we go any further, we obviously are aware of a picture floating around with the sign-stealer guy," he said. "Our people are doing everything they can to get to the bottom of it. ... I do know that his name was on none of the passes that were let out. Now we'll just keep tracing it back, and tracing it back, and try to figure it out. ... There's no place in football for that." At season's end, CMU had provided no updates to the credentialed mystery man's identity.

On Nov. 1, ESPN reported

that a majority of Big Ten coaches told Petitti during a video call that they were irked at the conference for not taking immediate action against Michigan. After 30 minutes of routine business, according to ESPN, Harbaugh left the call so other coaches could speak freely. They did so for an hour, ESPN said, using words such as "tainted," "fraudulent" and "unprecedented" in an intense and emotional session.

On Nov. 2, conference athletic directors called on Petitti to take action. ESPN wrote that "Haller worried about players potentially getting hurt because Michigan players, in theory, knew where they'd be going on plays."

Also on Nov. 2, Purdue coach Ryan Walters, his 2-6 team 32½-point underdogs to the Wolverines before their game that week, didn't hesitate to criticize U-M during his weekly radio show. "What's crazy is they

aren't allegations," he said. "It happened. There's video evidence. There's ticket purchases and sales that you can track back. We know for a fact that they were at a number of our games."

On Nov. 3, after Yahoo reported that Stalions had been fired, Michigan released a Friday night statement that he had resigned that afternoon. The Associated Press reported that Stalions failed to show up for a hearing and told U-M through his attorney that he would not cooperate in internal or external investigations.

Ten days later, after obtaining Stalions' personnel file through an open-records request, the *Detroit News* reported that Stalions was told Nov. 1 that a disciplinary review meeting was scheduled for the next day "to discuss your failure to cooperate" with a U-M and NCAA investigation and "termination of

employment may result from this conference."

Stalions' attorney, Brad Beckworth, told *The Athletic* that his client "hopes his resignation will help the team and coaching staff focus on tomorrow's game and the remainder of the season."

Beckworth added: "Connor also wants to make it clear that, to his knowledge, neither Coach Harbaugh, nor any other coach or staff member, told anyone to break any rules or were aware of improper conduct regarding the recent allegations of advanced scouting."

In his first public comments since the scandal broke, Stalions gave this statement to *The Athletic*:

"I love the University of Michigan and its football program. And I am extremely grateful for the opportunity I've had to work with the incredible student-athletes, Coach Harbaugh and the other coaches that have been a part of the Michigan football family during my tenure. I do not want to be a distraction from what I hope to be a championship run for the team, and I will continue to cheer them on."

On Nov. 4, a day after Petitti met with U-M president Santa Ono and Manuel in Ann Arbor, where the commissioner was attending the Big Ten field hockey tournament, ESPN reported that U-M could be punished within the next few days. ESPN also obtained an email that Ono sent to Petitti (and to other conference presidents and chancellors), urging the commissioner to respect due process and let the NCAA inquiry run its course.

Ono wrote he was "deeply concerned" about the allegations and U-M was "committed to ethics, integrity and fair play."

The Wolverines kicked off to Purdue at 7:33 p.m. Afterward, Harbaugh said of Ono's actions: "Deeply appreciate it."

After a week off, the Wolverines weren't sharp, but they still plowed through the Boilermakers standing on the tracks.

KIRTHMON F. DOZIER/DETROIT FREE PRESS

Sophomore tight end Colston Loveland put together another of those games that figured to land him on the All-Big Ten first team. He caught four passes from J.J. McCarthy for 55 yards — 17 yards, 12 yards, nine yards, 17 yards. Each reception moved the chains.

Runaway train

By Tony Garcia

THE BIG PICTURE

Plenty of questions remained for Michigan off the field, and perhaps a few more presented themselves on the field against Purdue.

For the ninth consecutive game, the Wolverines dismantled a vastly overmatched opponent. This time, a 41-13 thrashing of the lowly Boilermakers wasn't quite as crisp as recent beatdowns. It did set up a high-stakes clash at No. 11 Penn State in a week.

KIRTHMON F. DOZIER/DETROIT FREE PRESS

Coming off a bye week, Michigan wasn't quite as in sync as in other blowouts. Cornelius Johnson, for instance, caught only two passes for 39 yards even though he was targeted seven times.

"I was just so impressed with the squad tonight," coach Jim Harbaugh said. "A bunch of stalwarts."

Quarterback J.J. McCarthy was good, but just a tick off, as his Heisman Trophy campaign took a step back. McCarthy, who played until the final kneel-downs for the first time this season, completed 24 of 37 passes for a season-high 335 yards.

He had no touchdowns or interceptions.

He wasn't helped by at least four drops by pass catchers; however, Roman Wilson finished with nine receptions for 143 yards, each a career high.

"I just got to put the ball in the right spot where I can make it easy to make a catch," McCarthy said. "It wasn't my best day with my accuracy.

Missed a couple throws that I want back big time, but it's a good problem to have when you're putting up 41 points still."

The running game also struggled. U-M ran 30 times for 146 yards when adjusting for three sacks and a kneel-down, numbers that were boosted because of a 44-yard end-around touchdown by freshman wide receiver

Semaj Morgan. Blake Corum did the bulk of the work on the ground, but he had a hard time finding open lanes, running 15 times for 44 yards (2.9 a carry) and had just one run for more than five yards.

"Obviously, it's not to the standard we want as a run game," McCarthy said. "But we're going to do everything and anything to get that going. It's going to be huge in these next coming weeks."

That said, Corum still scored three times, bringing his nation-leading total to 16 rushing touchdowns. He moved into a second-place tie with Tyrone Wheatley at 47 rushing TDs on U-M's career list behind Anthony Thomas' 55.

Donovan Edwards also ran eight times for 21 yards and a score and caught three passes for 41 yards.

U-M entered the game leading the nation in scoring defense (5.9 points a game), total defense (227.8 yards) and passing defense (141.0 yards) and nearly improved on all of those numbers until Purdue's garbage-time touchdown after a 75-yard drive with 18 seconds left in the game. The Boilermakers gained 269 yards total and 144 through the air.

Cornerback Will Johnson, who made two interceptions against Purdue in the 2022 Big Ten championship game, came away with an early interception.

The only points the top unit allowed with the game in doubt — two second-quarter field goals — came when Purdue started drives inside U-M's 35. The Boilermakers' first six possessions ended with five punts and the interception.

U-M held Purdue's Hudson Card, a transfer from Texas, to 12 of 28 passing for 144 yards, a touchdown and an interception.

"It was a dominant performance," Harbaugh said. "I didn't see rust, I saw our guys were fresh, ready to play."

THE PREAMBLE

▶▶▶ Although NBC chose to show Michigan-Purdue in prime-time, nobody expected a close game. Despite an Air Raid offense, the Boilermakers were just another subpar squad from the Big Ten West with 2-6 overall and 1-4 conference records. Hired from Illinois for his defensive bona fides, first-year Purdue coach Ryan Walters already had five losses in which his team surrendered at least 31 points.

▶▶▶ On his weekly radio show, Walters didn't hide his contempt for the sign-stealing scandal and revealed his plan to skirt it. "We've had to teach our guys a new language in terms of some signals," he said, "and we'll operate differently offensively. You might see us in a huddle for the first time this season. So it is what it is."

▶▶▶ For Michigan, coming off its bye week, the game figured to be its last cakewalk before the homestretch that would define its season: at Penn State, at Maryland, vs. Ohio State. U-M was favored by 32½ points against Purdue.

Although the new kid on the block, Purdue's Ryan Walters pointed toward Ann Arbor and declared U-M guilty. His post-game handshake with Jim Harbaugh was a mid-field flyby. KIRTHMON F. DOZIER/DFP

THE PLAY-BY-PLAY

▶▶▶ On the game's first play, Purdue broke off a 10-yard run. The Boilermakers gained only 13 yards on their other 10 first-quarter plays. On its first drive, Michigan needed only six plays to cover 76 yards, capped by Blake Corum's two-yard touchdown run.

▶▶▶ After a Purdue three-and-out, Michigan needed seven plays to cover 67 yards, capped by Corum's three-yard scoring run. James Turner's 30-yard and 31-yard field goals gave U-M a 20-0 lead midway through the second quarter.

▶▶▶ The halftime score was 20-6 because Purdue kicked short field goals after a punt hit a U-M blocker in the back and Kale Mullings was stuffed on fourth-and-one. Each time, Purdue took over at the U-M 34.

KIRTHMON F. DOZIER/DETROIT FREE PRESS

Senior tailback Blake Corum added three more short touchdown runs to his resume, but his night was otherwise a slog. He needed 15 carries for 46 yards, and his two catches yielded three yards. He still led the country with 16 rushing touchdowns.

Sophomore cornerback Will Johnson continued to round into form. Besides tackling Purdue's Devin Mockobee, he made an interception and broke up two passes.
KIRTHMON F. DOZIER/DETROIT FREE PRESS

THE PRIME NUMBER

0

Number of plays Michigan's opponents had run inside the Wolverines' 10-yard line. The six touchdowns U-M had allowed covered, in order, a 20-yard run by UNLV, a 69-yard pass by Rutgers, a 74-yard run by Nebraska, a 35-yard pass by Minnesota, a 44-yard pass by Indiana and a 24-yard pass by Purdue.

THE PROCLAMATIONS

▶▶▶ **TAILBACK DONOVAN EDWARDS:** "We don't have to prove nothing to nobody."

▶▶▶ **ATHLETIC DIRECTOR WARDE MANUEL:** "I have nothing to say. I'm here to see Jim and celebrate this victory. ... Y'all can keep asking me all the questions you want, but I have no comment. ... It's just the choice I'm making."

▶▶▶ **COACH JIM HARBAUGH:** "The comments keep coming about why they're good, how they're good; they're all just good. ... I mean, just watch the game, turn on the tape. That's why they're so good. They're good at it."

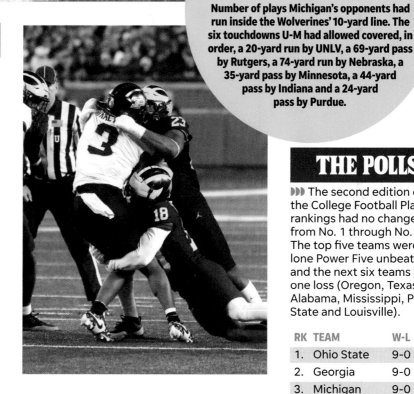

Linebacker Michael Barrett (No. 23) and defensive back Ja'Den McBurrows (No. 18) perfected the hit 'em high and hit 'em low technique to stop Purdue's Tyrone Tracy Jr. in his tracks.
KIRTHMON F. DOZIER/DETROIT FREE PRESS

THE POLLS

▶▶▶ The second edition of the College Football Playoff rankings had no changes from No. 1 through No. 8. The top five teams were the lone Power Five unbeatens, and the next six teams had one loss (Oregon, Texas, Alabama, Mississippi, Penn State and Louisville).

RK	TEAM	W-L	PVS
1.	Ohio State	9-0	1
2.	Georgia	9-0	2
3.	Michigan	9-0	3
4.	Florida State	9-0	4
5.	Washington	9-0	5

▶▶▶ The top 10 in the US LBM coaches poll and the AP media poll were identical: Georgia, Michigan, OSU, FSU, Washington, Oregon, Texas, Alabama, Penn State, Mississippi.

THE PRESS BOX

▶▶▶ **SHAWN WINDSOR, DETROIT FREE PRESS:** "They want to prove they are winning because of their talent, because they are good at football. Which means they must keep winning, and hope that their play makes the loudest statement of all, eventually quieting everything else."

▶▶▶ **RAINER SABIN, DETROIT FREE PRESS:** "For 3½ hours, inside the maize-and-blue cocoon, it looked like nothing could stop them. But who knows what awaits Michigan and its fans outside the Big House's walls? That uncomfortable reality, unfortunately, appears inescapable."

(NON-) CRIME &
PUNISHMENT

RICK OSENTOSKI/USA TODAY SPORTS

As he coached against Purdue at Michigan Stadium, Jim Harbaugh likely wondered when he would coach on the sidelines again. He knew the Big Ten wanted to suspend him, his side was open to a legal challenge and the next week might be a rollercoaster.

With a sudden strike, the Big Ten brought the hammer down on the Wolverines — and coach Jim Harbaugh.

By Gene Myers

Five days before the game that could represent the entire season — all the championship hopes and dreams, the blood, sweat and jeers, and Michigan vs. Everybody merch ...

Likely fewer than five days before the Big Ten would decide whether to punish the Wolverines over the sign-stealing firestorm after its football coaches and athletic directors demanded frontier justice ...

Michigan geared up for a trip to Penn State.

Before the season opener, J.J. McCarthy turned his shirt into a makeshift "Free Harbaugh" sign. On Nov. 11, plenty of homemade signs popped up in Happy Valley. Michigan's coach wouldn't have seen them because he was not allowed near Beaver Stadium.

So how did Jim Harbaugh open his weekly news conference? He took a swig of pop, placed the can under the podium and addressed the media with enthusiasm unknown to mankind.

"Big game atmosphere in Schembechler Hall, a ton of enthusiasm and excitement, and my energy level was already sky high, but then I got a visit from the Nature Boy, Ric Flair, very close friend," Harbaugh said as his voice deepened and his volume rose. "And that just brought the enthusiasm to a new level."

Columnist Jeff Seidel wrote in the *Free Press*: "It was a bizarre press conference, even by Harbaugh standards. ... This is Michigan: Everything feels strange right now."

Flair was perhaps the greatest pro wrestler in his day, one who embraced the moniker of The Dirtiest Player in the Game. While Harbaugh talked about him — and the unbeaten Nittany Lions — behind the scenes Michigan officials were trying their hardest to ensure Harbaugh would be on the sidelines at Happy Valley.

On this Monday in early November, Michigan confirmed that the Big Ten recently sent a formal notice regarding potential disciplinary action under the conference's sportsmanship policy. The school was given until Wednesday to file its response. Later Monday, athletic director Warde Manuel issued a statement that he would not travel to Dallas for the weekly meeting of the College Football Playoff selection committee so he could attend "to important matters regarding the ongoing investigation into our football team."

Yahoo! Sports reported that commissioner Tony Petitti had laid out the possibility of a multigame suspension for Harbaugh during Petitti's meeting with Manuel and U-M president Santa Ono the previous Friday. Yahoo also reported that the NCAA had supplied the Big Ten with its preliminary findings, which Yahoo's sources said did not include direct evidence linking Harbaugh to a sign-stealing scheme. Ono and Manuel pushed back, requesting due process by waiting for the NCAA to finish its business. Among the options on the table were for U-M to seek a temporary restraining order against the conference if Harbaugh were suspended.

Under the sportsmanship policy, Petitti had "exclusive authority" to mete out discipline to those who violate the "integrity of the competition" in the "competitive arena." On his own, Petitti could deliver "standard" penalties, such as admonishment, reprimand, fines not in excess of $10,000 and suspensions no longer than two games. To level "major" penalties, which would be anything that exceeded the standard penalties, Petitti would need the approval of the Joint Group Executive Committee, comprised of senior officials from across the conference's schools.

On Wednesday, Michigan submitted a biting and aggressive 10-page response to the Big Ten. Also included were two documents of U-M's offensive and defensive signs allegedly stolen and shared by other conference teams and an eight-page letter from Harbaugh's attorney, Tom Mars, who had been his counsel during the initial NCAA investigation. Yahoo obtained copies of the documents and reported their contents Thursday.

In a nutshell, U-M told Petitti that he was overstepping his authority, rushing to judgment because of public and internal pressure, and denying U-M due process spelled out in the conference handbook. U-M argued that the conference's sportsmanship policy had never been "deployed as a backdoor way of holding an institution or individual responsible for a rule violation" and that the conference's rules did not recognize the NCAA's head coach responsibility bylaw in which a boss was responsible for all actions of his subordinates.

U-M questioned much of the evidence presented by the conference and charged that the conference alluded to evidence it did not share.

In the letter, U-M said it would "accept responsibility for what a full investigation will fairly show" about the actions by Connor Stalions, argued though that he was a one-man operation and insisted there was no evidence other coaches, most notably Harbaugh, knew what methods he used to obtain information. Plus, U-M questioned whether any rules were broken by Stalions' associates because they weren't "athletics personnel" and whether recording games on a devices violated an NCAA prohibition because it applied to "field equipment deployed during games in which that institution participates."

"We are not aware of any evidence or allegations suggesting that violations are ongoing now that Stalions is no longer part of the football

MATTHEW O'HAREN/USA TODAY SPORTS

Sorry, Penn State fans, you were late to the "Don't Steal My Sign" party. Only one question remained: Would these now-cliché signs greet the Wolverines at road venues for years or decades?

program, or that there are any other circumstances of ongoing or irreparable harm requiring or justifying immediate or interim sanctions," U-M said in the letter, which was signed by Manuel.

U-M also warned Petitti to watch what precedents he might set "given the reality that in-person scouting, collusion among opponents and other questionable practices may well be far more prevalent than believed."

The Big Ten's response? Balderdash! In a 13-page letter to Manuel, Petitti shot down U-M's arguments and suspended Harbaugh for the last three games of the regular season, although he could continue coaching at practices.

The Wolverines' response? Flippin' furious. And not just

because of the suspension.

Among their gripes: The Big Ten's announcement came while the team was flying to Penn State. U-M wasn't alerted first. (Harbaugh found out via social media, when someone reached over his shoulder to show him the news on a phone.) The decision came down on a Friday afternoon on a federal holiday, limiting U-M's ability to pursue legal action.

From the team plane, J.J. McCarthy and several other players tweeted a single word: bet. It became another mantra for the season's homestretch. The team wasn't using the word in a gambling sense. In popular slang, according to Dictionary.com, bet meant "affirmation, agreement or approval along the lines of 'cool!' or 'I'm

down!'" But bet also could mean "you can count on it" or "trust me." The players used it to acknowledge the suspension of their coach and to tell the college football world they were locked and loaded for the rest of the season. *Free Press* columnist Shawn Windsor described it as: "Doubt us at your peril!" By early 2024, McCarthy's one-word tweet, sent at 5:14 p.m. on Nov. 10, had been viewed more than 24.8 million times, including by Tom Brady, according to X's analytics.

(Harbaugh eventually started saying bet, too. "Our players came up with this 'bet! bet!'" he said during the College Football Playoff selection show. "I even had to look up what it means. But what it means to me is 'Bringing Everyone Together,' and that's

MATTHEW O'HAREN/USA TODAY SPORTS

Offensive coordinator Sherrone Moore roamed the field during the early warmups. When he arrived at Beaver Stadium, Michigan still had some hope for a temporary restraining order.

what our team has done. So, bet!")

The Big Ten found U-M in violation of its sportsmanship policy "for conducting an impermissible, in-person scouting operation over multiple years, resulting in an unfair competitive advantage that comprised the integrity of competition."

In his letter, Petitti said U-M's response "does not deny that the impermissible scheme occurred. Instead, it offers only procedural and technical arguments designed to delay accountability." He also wrote that "the existence of the impermissible scheme is proven."

Petitti, though, admitted the conference had no evidence of wrongdoing by Harbaugh.

"We impose this disciplinary action even though the conference has not yet received any information indicating that head football coach Harbaugh was aware

of the impermissible nature of the sign-stealing scheme," Petitti wrote. "This is not a sanction of Coach Harbaugh. It is a sanction against the university that, under the extraordinary circumstances presented by this offensive conduct, best fits the violation because: 1) it preserves the ability of the university's football student-athletes to continue competing; and 2) it recognizes that the head coach embodies the university for purposes of its football program."

Michigan responded swiftly on two fronts: through harsh rhetoric and by filing for a temporary restraining order.

"Today's action by commissioner Petitti ... violates basic tenets of due process," a statement released by U-M said in part. "We are dismayed at the commissioner's rush to judgment when there is an ongoing NCAA investigation — one in which we are fully cooperating."

U-M's request to stay the suspension was filed with Washtenaw County Circuit Judge Timothy Connors, also a lecturer at U-M's law school.

According to Petitti's letter, the NCAA "knew and could prove" the following: that Stalions "participated and co-ordinated a vast off-campus, in-person, advance scouting scheme; that Stalions bought and forwarded game tickets for future U-M opponents; and that Stalions and others recorded signs of other teams while at those games.

U-M's attempt at a legal Hail Mary, in a 219-page filing by the Board of Regents and Harbaugh, failed late Saturday morning when the judge decided not to rule and scheduled a hearing for the following Friday. A police escort had been on standby to whisk Harbaugh to Beaver Stadium at the last minute.

Instead, the reins were passed to Sherrone Moore, the offensive coordinator

and offensive line coach who served as acting head coach for a 31-6 victory over Bowling Green in September.

Before the high noon kick-off between the third-ranked Wolverines and 10th-ranked Nittany Lions, Manuel provided the last bit of pregame dramatics. He released a blistering, lengthy statement about the conference's decision. The harsh tone caught the vast media contingent at the game off guard and drew a fair share of criticism.

Part of the statement:

"Under the guise of the NCAA rule regarding head coach responsibility, the Big Ten decided to penalize Coach Harbaugh without knowing all the facts, and I find that completely unethical, insulting to a well-established process within the NCAA, and an assault on the rights of everyone (especially in the Big Ten) to be judged by a fair and complete investigation. Not liking someone or another university or believing without any evidence that they knew or saying someone should have known without an investigation is not grounds to remove someone from their position before the NCAA process has reached a conclusion through a full NCAA investigative process.

"All of the head coaches in the Big Ten (some who have been accused of actively participating in the trading of signals of opponents) and my Big Ten AD colleagues can rejoice today that someone was 'held accountable,' but they should be worried about the new standard of judgment (without complete investigation) that has been unleashed in this conference.

"You may have removed him from our sidelines today, but Jim Harbaugh is our head football coach. We look forward to defending Jim's right to coach our football team at the hearing on Friday."

The Nittany Lions kicked off to Michigan at 12:06 p.m.

Suddenly without their head coach (again), the Wolverines hunkered down and kept to the ground in Happy Valley.

MATTHEW O'HAREN/USA TODAY SPORTS

Penn State's Kevin Winston led all tacklers with 12, but he had no chance to run down Blake Corum when Corum could taste the sweet nectar of the end zone. With 4:15 left, right after PSU failed on a fourth down, Corum ripped off a 30-yard touchdown for a 24-9 U-M lead.

Valley forged

By Rainer Sabin
THE BIG PICTURE

Crimson splotches were visible on his cheeks. There was a piece of tape affixed to the bridge of his nose, reddened by the blood that oozed from a nasty cut that opened during a rousing 24-15 victory over Penn State in this hilly burg of Central Pennsylvania.

This was the gnarled face of Blake Corum and perhaps Michigan football, too. But here he was, still standing after the biggest fight yet this season. So, too, were the Wolverines following a week when the program waged battles on multiple fronts and was dealt some major blows.

J.J. McCarthy used his golden arm for only eight passes — seven of which he completed — but he couldn't have cared less. "One of our strengths," he said, "is to be able to adapt to what the defense is giving us." His passes gained 60 yards, his legs gained 34.

Donovan Edwards turned on the jets and pulled away from Kevin Winston for a 22-yard rushing touchdown in the second quarter. It gave Michigan its first two-score advantage at 14-3.

None was greater than Big Ten commissioner Tony Petitti's decision to ban Jim Harbaugh from the sideline for the rest of the regular season. The suspension infuriated the Wolverines.

"Pissed off a lot of guys," captain Trevor Keegan said.

Then, 90 minutes before game time, word came down that a ruling on the court order wouldn't be made in time for Harbaugh to coach, forcing offensive coordinator Sherrone Moore to step in as his replacement.

"Crazy 24 hours," Moore said. "But at the same time, our team is built for this."

It certainly seemed that way. Harbaugh molded the Wolverines into a powerful legion that could destroy their opponents, defy their skeptics, answer their critics and please their supporters. They did all the above at Happy Valley, where they unleashed their fury on the 10th-ranked Nittany Lions and pummeled them into submission.

In a game that represented Michigan's first true test of the season, the third-ranked Wolverines channeled their embattled coach's spirit by winning the old-fashioned way with a relentless rushing attack and an unyielding defense. After initially giving Heisman Trophy contender J.J. McCarthy another stab at carrying U-M by air, Moore and the rest of Harbaugh's

On his decisive 30-yard touchdown, which came on an inside zone run, Blake Corum hesitated behind the line, watched his hole open and then ran untouched. "Safety took a bad angle," he said. "And that was it."
MATTHEW O'HAREN/ USA TODAY SPORTS

trusted aides turned this contest into a vintage Big Ten rock fight.

It was a brilliant schematic maneuver considering Penn State's blitz-happy defensive coordinator, Manny Diaz, went after McCarthy from the beginning and hit his target on occasion. The best way to neutralize a pass rush, Michigan's brain trust concluded, was to stop throwing the ball. So, the Wolverines didn't.

McCarthy unleashed only one pass in the second half and it didn't even count, negated by an interference penalty. Michigan instead relied on Corum and Donovan Edwards to sap Penn State's will and blunt its ferocity. The Wolverines' final 30 plays — not counting kicks and kneel-downs —were runs, and a ground

attack that spent most of this fall producing uneven results revved up to become their supercharged engine.

Corum reprised his role from 2022 as U-M's reliable dynamo, gaining 145 yards and scoring two touchdowns on 26 attempts. His 23rd carry, a 30-yard sprint to the end zone with roughly four minutes left, was his piece de resistance. It broke Penn State once and for all, applying the exclamation point to Michigan's latest bold statement.

As the student section began to empty, Corum watched with delight.

"We were able to quiet them down throughout the game but especially at the end," Corum said.

The sound of silence was welcomed by a team that had been subjected to lots of

noise in recent weeks as the sign-stealing scandal had become the talk of the sport, echoing wherever the Wolverines went.

It had invited suspicion about U-M's recent return to prominence, which had been marked by a run of 35 victories in its last 38 games and 22 straight in a league where they now were seen as renegades by their Big Ten companions. It had detracted from the Wolverines' pursuit of a national title, casting a pall over that quest. It had caused U-M's players, a cohort of 18- to 23-year-olds, to face uncomfortable questions and respond to demeaning accusations.

"We take it to heart, man," Keegan said. "The players who have been here for a while, we did everything we

could to turn this program around and bring it back to where Michigan needs to be. ... We know who we are."

So did everyone else. Their admirers and haters could agree these Wolverines were a tough bunch with a collective resolve that was as rare as it was impressive.

It was on display when Corum led the charge. Wounded but undeterred, he told his teammates in the huddle to keep scrapping and clawing. "Fight, fight, fight," he implored.

The Wolverines did so under extraordinary circumstances, and in the end, they were still standing. They might have been bloodied, bruised, mangled and maimed. But they were still undefeated in the place where it counted most: in the arena.

DAN RAINVILLE/USA TODAY SPORTS

Social media went crazy when Michigan started using flags, placards and whatnot to shield their huddles near the sideline. Were the Wolverines afraid of stolen signs? Were they trolling critics?

THE PREAMBLE

▶▶▶ Michigan's hopes for a third straight berth in the College Football Playoff and possibly a third straight Big Ten title were riding on the outcome of the high noon shootout with Penn State, which had only lost to Ohio State. Only nobody expected a shootout. These teams were built on defense. Scoring defense: No. 1 U-M (6.7 points), No. 3 PSU (12.5). Total defense: No. 1 U-M (232.3 yards), No. 2 PSU (246.3). Rushing defense: No. 1 PSU (55.9), No. 11 U-M (91.0). Passing defense: No. 1 U-M (141.3), No. 21 PSU (190.4). Only 21st? PSU made up for it with the second-highest sack total in the country. U-M was favored by 5½ points.

▶▶▶ Nittany Lions coach James Franklin didn't take the bait when asked to comment about the sign-stealing scandal. "I'm focused on all the stuff I see on film," he said. "That's what we're focused on, is all the stuff that we see on film, their players, their scheme."

▶▶▶ For the fourth time in 10 games the Wolverines would play without coach Jim Harbaugh on the sideline.

THE PLAY-BY-PLAY

▶▶▶ Penn State became the first team to run a play inside Michigan's 10-yard line. Its second drive produced a first-and-goal from the U-M 3. Then Michael Barrett stuffed Kaytron Allen for no gain, Mason Graham pressured Drew Allar into an incompletion and Will Johnson broke up a pass in the end zone. A 20-yard field gave Penn State a 3-0 lead with 2:17 left in the first quarter.

▶▶▶ Michigan answered with touchdowns on its next two drives: a three-yard run by Blake Corum and a 22-yard run by Donovan Edwards. In the final minute of the half, Allar scored on an 11-yard run, but his two-point pass failed. So U-M led, 14-9, at halftime.

▶▶▶ Penn State didn't score again until the last two minutes of the game. By then, U-M had built a 24-9 lead on a 22-yard James Turner field goal in the third quarter and a 30-yard Corum run with 4:15 left in the fourth quarter.

▶▶▶ The Wolverines rushed the ball 46 times for 227

DAN RAINVILLE/USA TODAY SPORTS

Penn State's Kobe King crumbled him on this play, but Blake Corum grinded out 26 carries for 145 yards. "Going into halftime," he said, "it was up front, we're going to dominate. I just kept preaching to them, 'Just push, just fight, fight, fight' and something's going to break, and that's what happened."

yards (4.9 a carry). J.J. McCarthy completed seven of his eight passes for 60 yards.

▶▶▶ The Nittany Lions managed only 238 total yards, including 74 through the air on 11 of 23 passing. The

next day, Franklin fired his offensive coordinator, Mike Yurcich.

Michigan's defense bedeviled quarterback Drew Allar and his entire offense. "The best defense in the country," acting head coach Sherrone Moore said. "They play fast up front, we see it in practice, it's a pain in the butt to block, it's hard to get open."
MATTHEW O'HAREN/ USA TODAY SPORTS

THE PRESS BOX

▶▶▶ **MITCH ALBOM, DETROIT FREE PRESS:** "Faced with their season — and their legacy — on the line, this Michigan team did what Michigan teams before them have historically done best. They ran. They ran again. And then, to mix things up, they ran some more."

▶▶▶ **SHAWN WINDSOR, DETROIT FREE PRESS:** "The stain of accusation isn't going away for these Wolverines. Not anytime soon. And that's a shame, because these players continue to show how special they can be. Besides, they have done nothing wrong."

▶▶▶ **TONY GARCIA, DETROIT FREE PRESS:** "Is there a grade better than A+? We'd like to give that if possible. All U-M did was go on the road in front of 110,856 fans — the second-largest crowd in Beaver Stadium history — and snatch their souls by winning a game without passing for the final 36 minutes and 14 seconds."

Penn State applied great pressure early — this sack by Dani Dennis-Sutton on J.J. McCarthy ended U-M's first possession.
DAN RAINVILLE/ USA TODAY SPORTS

THE PROCLAMATIONS

▶▶▶ **QUARTERBACK J.J. MCCARTHY:** "Best offensive line in the country, two of the best backs in the country, we just gotta take what the defense is giving us, so we adapted and we adjusted."

▶▶▶ **ACTING HEAD COACH SHERRONE MOORE:** "It was positive gain after positive gain. Those three and fours turn into 15 and 16 and then all of a sudden it's a 40-yarder. ... Adding seven offensive linemen, that's a wrinkle we had for a little while."

▶▶▶ **PENN STATE COACH JAMES FRANKLIN:** "We've lost to the No. 1 and the No. 3 team in the country. That's not good enough. We have to find ways to win those games."

MATTHEW O'HAREN/USA TODAY SPORTS

Tailback Blake Corum, bleeding from the bridge of his nose, and acting head coach Sherrone Moore, sobbing and swearing simultaneously, made for great television during Jenny Taft's interview. Corum later said: "We wanted to go out there, fight for Michigan, fight for each other and fight for Coach Harbaugh."

THE POSTSCRIPT

▶▶▶ Moments after two J.J. McCarthy kneeldowns, Fox's Jenny Taft grabbed Moore for a quick word with the victorious coach. Too overcome with emotion to talk for several seconds, as tears flowed down his face, Moore thanked the Lord and then thanked Harbaugh.

▶▶▶ "(Expletive) love you, man," he said while sobbing. "Love the (expletive) out of you, man. Did this for you." He hesitated for an instant. "For this university, the president, our AD. We got the best players, best university, best alumni in the country. Love you, guys!"

▶▶▶ Then Moore turned toward Corum, who had blood between his eyebrows, waiting for his turn to chat with Taft. Moore was breathing and sobbing heavily. And he was fired up.

▶▶▶ "These (expletive) guys right here, these guys right here, man," he blurted out. "These guys did it! These guys did it, man!"

▶▶▶ Moore slapped hands with Corum and threw an arm around him. As Moore headed off to celebrate, Moore told Taft to "talk to him, man" and added a "love you."

MATTHEW O'HAREN/USA TODAY SPORTS

On the field, in the locker room, at the airport and at home, Sherrone Moore gave and received countless hugs for a job well done at Happy Valley.

THE PRIME NUMBER

3

Points scored by Michigan in the third quarter, the first points surrendered by Penn State in that quarter during the season. U-M had yet to allow a third-quarter point.

THE POLLS

▶▶▶ The third edition of the College Football Playoff rankings saw Georgia pass Ohio State for the No. 1 ranking after the Bulldogs blitzed Mississippi, 52-17. There were no changes from Nos. 3 to 8. The top five teams were the lone Power Five unbeatens, and the next three teams had one loss (Oregon, Texas, Alabama).

RK	TEAM	W-L	PVS
1.	Georgia	10-0	2
2.	Ohio State	10-0	1
3.	Michigan	10-0	3
4.	Florida State	10-0	4
5.	Washington	10-0	5

▶▶▶ The top 10 in the US LBM coaches poll and the AP media poll were identical: Georgia, Michigan, OSU, FSU, Washington, Oregon, Texas, Alabama, Louisville, Oregon State.

ONE GRAND VICTORY!

The Wolverines (with plenty of fans in the background) pose for posterity after capturing the 1,000th victory in Michigan's 144 years of playing football. The milestone came Nov. 18, 2023, at SECU Stadium in College Park, Maryland. U-M beat the Terrapins, 31-24.

Inside the Wolverines' journey from a challenge match in Chicago to their historic 1,000th football victory.

By Ryan Ford

It all started with a bit of trash talk.

A few sporting students at Racine College in Wisconsin challenged the superiority of Michigan's student body at the game of "foot-ball," a soccer-like sport sweeping the nation a decade after its introduction to the college landscape — Rutgers beat Princeton, 6-4, in New Brunswick, New Jersey, on Nov. 6, 1869.

After a bit of dawdling, the first group of maize-and-blue ambassadors visited Chicago in May 1879 to show what the Wolverines had been practicing since 1873.

The Wolverines dominated the Purple Stockings (as Racine was known then) by the epic score of ... 1-0.

The victory kicked off 144 years of Michigan football and paved the way for victory No. 1,000 on Nov. 18, 2023. On that Saturday afternoon at Maryland, with a 31-24 triumph, the Wolverines became the first collegiate, professional or prep team to win — in money terms — a grand.

Closest in the collegiate ranks that day were Ohio State (964 victories), Alabama (963) and Notre Dame and Texas (each with 946). Closest in the prep ranks were Valdosta High in Georgia (952) and Male High in Louisville, Kentucky (948).

Closest in the pro ranks were the Green Bay Packers (829, including 36 in the playoffs).

Michigan needed 87 seasons to reach 500 victories, but just 56 more to climb to 1,000 (despite the 21st Century dark ages of Rich Rodriguez and Brady Hoke). By Nov. 18, 2023, the Wolverines also had picked up 44 conference championships, 11 national titles, three Heisman Trophies and a couple of sign-stealing scandals (including allegedly being burgled by University of Chicago legend Amos Alonzo Stagg in 1894).

The pursuit of 1,000 victories picked up speed with the arrival of Bo Schembechler in 1969 and his ensuing coaching tree that featured Gary Moeller (1990-94), Lloyd Carr (1995-2007) and Jim Harbaugh (2015-23). The Wolverines went from the fifth NCAA program to win 600 games (in 1978) to the second to win 800 games (in 2000) to the first to win 900 (in 2012).

A look at 16 milestone victories for the Victors Valiant on the journey to No. 1,000:

001 MAY 30, 1879
U-M 1, RACINE 0

Ann Arbor might have been a football-mad town, but the rest of the region was less so. A preview of the game in the Chicago Tribune called it "foot-ball" and noted that "this will be the first game of Rugby foot-ball ever played in Chicago, and its novelty should insure a large attendance." Indeed, 500 fans were on hand at White-Stocking Park — what's now called Millennium Park in downtown Chicago — to see Michigan take on Racine in the first intercollegiate game played west of the Allegheny Mountains. Irving Kane Pond scored U-M's lone touchdown early in the match, but the sport's rules at the time awarded points only for kicks, not TDs. Captain Dave Detar booted the ball through the goalposts for the Wolverines' lone score of the year.

003 MAY 12, 1883
U-M 40, DETROIT IND. 5

Despite its inaugural intercollegiate success, it took awhile for Michigan to get a victory in Ann Arbor. U-M's second game was a scoreless tie with the University of Toronto at Detroit on Nov. 1, 1879, and the Wolverines followed up with a 13-6 triumph at Toronto on Nov. 5, 1880. But 1881 brought three losses — on the road at Harvard, Yale and Princeton over five days — and 1882 featured no games. Finally, in 1883, captain William Olcott's squad beat Detroit Independents under new scoring rules: Touchdowns and point-after kicks were worth four points apiece, while field goals delivered five points.

050 NOV. 29, 1894
U-M 6, CHICAGO 4

U-M capped its first nine-victory season — in its fourth season with at least nine games played — with a thrilling road victory over the University of Chicago (a charter member of what would become the Big Ten, although now more famous for being one of the birthplaces of nuclear science). The *Free Press*' front-page coverage noted "from the noise it seemed as if pandemonium had been turned loose" in the crowd of 6,000. Chicago took an early lead, on an early version of the Brotherly Shove 11 minutes in, but missed the ensuing two-point kick. U-M struggled to run throughout, with Stagg's Maroons clogging the middle seemingly every time the Wolverines attempted runs there and punching balls loose for fumbles on several long gains. The Wolverines finally found the winning formula in the second half, driving to Chicago's 5. From there, Gustave Ferbert (who would go on to coach U-M from 1897-99) took the ball to the end zone on an end around, and John Bloomingston made the kick for the lead, followed by a late Michigan defensive stand on its 20. Then came a bit of intrigue four days later. In a twist that should sound familiar, there were accusations of stealing signs. The *Michigan Daily* alleged that Stagg had learned the Wolverines' signals by umpiring U-M's victory over Oberlin and attending a game in Detroit against Cornell with at least two of his players. "Chicago knew all but a few of Michigan's plays and would mass to meet them," the *Daily* wrote. "Whether there is a traitor in Michigan's camp or Stagg learned the signals matters not — Chicago was unsportsmanlike enough to make use of them."

THE DECADES

The Wolverines have won at least 90 games in three different 10-year spans, topped by the 96 for Bo Schembechler's squads in the 1970s:

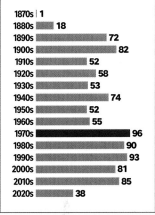

Decade	Wins
1870s	1
1880s	18
1890s	72
1900s	82
1910s	52
1920s	58
1930s	53
1940s	74
1950s	52
1960s	55
1970s	96
1980s	90
1990s	93
2000s	81
2010s	85
2020s	38

069
OCT. 16, 1897
U-M 34, OHIO STATE 0

Like in so many years to come, the Wolverines' season was blown up by a disappointing finish against a school from Ohio. In 1897, it was Ohio Wesleyan, which played U-M to a scoreless tie on Oct. 9. The following week, the Wolverines got their revenge against That School Down South by scoring six touchdowns (for four points apiece, with three scored by G.D. Stuart) and five PATs (for two points apiece, all by captain James Hogg) in just the first half, which lasted 20 minutes. The second half was even shorter — 15 minutes — as the Wolverines didn't "find any great difficulty in gaining either around Ohio's ends or through the line, while Ohio could do nothing with the few chances it had to play an offensive game," according to the *Free Press*' account.

THE COACHES

Just five head coaches — Bo Schembechler, Fielding Yost, Lloyd Carr, Jim Harbaugh and Fritz Crisler — accounted for 63.7% of Michigan's first 1,000 victories:

 **5. FRITZ CRISLER** *71*

 **4. JIM HARBAUGH** *85*

 **3. LLOYD CARR** *122*

 **2. FIELDING YOST** *165*

1. BO SCHEMBECHLER *194*

076 — OCT. 12, 1898 — U-M 39, M.A.C. 0

A 10-0 season in which Michigan won its first Western Conference championship included its first of 73 victories over the school that would become Michigan State. In what became a frequent refrain in the rivalry, U-M displayed "a lack of aggressiveness when the farmers had the ball," according to the *Free Press*' account of the Wednesday game, played in two 20-minute halves. The Wolverines, though, put up six TDs — worth five points apiece — plus four PAT kicks and, for the first time in U-M history … a field goal! Leo Keena connected on a placekick from 23 yards out — worth five points — in the second half, "the first time a Michigan 11 has ever scored in that fashion," according to the *Free Press*.

100 — OCT. 5, 1901 — U-M 57, CASE 0

There's just something about schools from Ohio that bring out a rivalry, as was the case with a visit to Ann Arbor from the Cleveland-based school that had lost to U-M in 1899 (28-6) and 1900 (24-6). Case insisted on changing one of the officials just before the game and demanded 20-minute halves, rather than the usual 30 minutes. When U-M objected, the Case players began to ride off in their carriages, forcing Michigan to agree to the altered format. The standoff blew up in Case's faces. "Their rather babyish action aroused the bleachers and nerved the Michigan men to play harder than would have been the case otherwise," the *Free Press* wrote. The Wolverines racked up 10 touchdowns (then worth five points apiece) and seven PAT kicks (worth one point each) and, in the second half against a worn-down squad, "runs of from 20 to 35 yards became very common." Coach Fielding Yost expressed the tone of the day with his postgame comment: "I am glad they stayed and that we licked them as hard as we did." Case might have gotten off easy: Yost's first squad at Michigan won all 11 of its games while outscoring opponents, 550-0 — including a 128-0 wipeout of Buffalo on Oct. 26, an 89-0 triumph over Beloit on Nov. 23 and a 49-0 victory over Stanford on Jan. 1, 1902, in the first Rose Bowl. Years later, the NCAA recognized the Wolverines as national champions, although Harvard also lays claim to the crown.

200 — OCT. 9, 1915 — U-M 35, MOUNT UNION 0

Despite the final score, this wasn't another blowout of an overmatched foe from Ohio. The Purple Raiders got their licks in everywhere but the end zone at Ferry Field. They stunned the Wolverines with an aggressive short passing game and drove deep into U-M territory several times. The *Free Press* reported: "The speedy scrappy collegians showed Michigan more things about the forward pass than the slower Wolverines ever dreamed of." When the Wolverines had the ball, though, Mount Union had few answers for punishing halfback John Maulbetsch, who had three touchdowns, plus a 37-yard run that set him up for a one-yard scoring run. Although only 5-feet-7 and 153 pounds, Maulbetsch made All-America as a sophomore in 1914 and was inducted into the College Football Hall of Fame in 1973, 23 years after his death. Among his nicknames as a noted line-plunger were the Featherweight Fullback and the Human Bullet. The remainder of the 1915 schedule was painful for U-M, which finished with three losses and a tie in its ninth season after exiting the Western Conference. The Wolverines rejoined in 1917.

THE FOES

The teams Michigan beat the most in its first 1,000 victories, within the Big Ten and outside of it:

BIG TEN

 4. ILLINOIS *62*

 3. INDIANA *71*

 2. MSU *73*

 1. MINN. *77*

NONCONFERENCE

 3. VANDY *10*

 3. EMU *10*

 2. N.D. *25*

 1. CASE *26*

The Big House didn't need to be so big when it opened in 1927.
DETROIT FREE PRESS ARCHIVES

270 OCT. 1, 1927
U-M 33, OHIO WESLEYAN 0

Just as the Wolverines opened Michigan Stadium, so too did the clouds open up, making for a water-logged performance at the (not-so) Big House. The listed attendance was 17,483, but newspaper accounts put the crowd at about 40,000 in the 84,401 capacity structure, despite a "wide open" north section, according to the Free Press, which also noted "in the populated areas many vacant seats appeared here and there." On the field, U-M took to the air thanks to relaxed rules on passing: LaVerne (Kip) Taylor scored the stadium's first TD on a 28-yard pass from Louis Gilbert in the first quarter. Gilbert, who scored or passed for all five Michigan touchdowns, took advantage of the wet conditions; he opened the second half with an 85-yard kickoff return for a touchdown — with the final two yards gained as he slid on the wet grass during the tackle. Gilbert also delivered three PATs, with one miss and one blocked. Seventy years after the game, nearing his 90th birthday, Taylor recounted his historic touchdown: "Louis Gilbert, our triple-threat man, looked at me and said, 'Listen, sophomore, if I throw it to you, you better catch it.' Well, the ball was so perfect I could have caught it in my teeth. I came across ... and there were two players coming at me. I sidestepped one, stiff-armed the other and ran into the corner."

300 OCT. 1, 1932
U-M 26, MICHIGAN STATE 0

In a rivalry Michigan had dominated for a quarter-century, these teams met after playing to scoreless ties the prior two seasons. They wouldn't become Big Ten foes for another 21 years. This game — the season opener U-M — featured a daunting "aerial attack" from the Wolverines, per the Free Press' next-day headline. Quarterback Harry Newman, a triple threat as a passer, runner and kicker, set up several scores with quick throws, and the Wolverines piled up 341 total yards. Newman threw 20 passes, seven that were completed and two that were intercepted. More impressive was the Michigan defense, which held the Spartans to 35 yards and no plays within U-M's 45 and forced 18 punts. The victory kicked off a national championship season for the Wolverines, who outscored their eight foes, 123-13. Newman made All-America and won the Douglas Fairbanks Award, a precursor to the Heisman Trophy. "Newman stood well above the mass," wrote Grantland Rice, a sports writing legend.

400 OCT. 23, 1948
U-M 27, MINNESOTA 14

The Wolverines entered this Little Brown Jug battle in Minneapolis having won 18 straight. No. 19 wasn't the prettiest of efforts; top-ranked Michigan went scoreless in the first quarter, then fell behind 1:16 into the second when punt returner Gene Derricotte fumbled and 245-pound Minnesota tackle Leo Nomellini (a future Pro Football Hall of Famer) fell on it in the end zone. The Wolverines struck quickly near the end of the half, scoring two TDs in the final 2:39, only for the 13th-ranked Golden Gophers to answer with a nine-play, 77-yard TD drive in the third quarter. But U-M claimed the lead for good later in the quarter on a freakish passing play — one of 11 completions (in a season-high 24 attempts) for 261 yards. On second-and-10 from the Gophers' 38, U-M's Chuck Ortmann found receiver Dick Rifenburg open at the 25; the future All-America made it 10 yards before a hit popped the ball free and started bouncing toward the end zone. Still on his feet, Rifenburg caught up to it, scooped it up and rumbled in for a TD. Finishing the season 9-0, the Wolverines captured their 10th national championship; the 11th didn't arrive until 1997. Their victory streak reached 25 games before ending against Army on Oct. 8, 1949 — the third-longest streak in program history (behind a 29-gamer in 1901-03 and a 26-gamer in 1903-05).

Chuck Ortmann was inducted into the Rose Bowl Hall of Fame in 2008.
DETROIT FREE PRESS ARCHIVES

Ron Johnson

500
NOV. 11, 1967
U-M 21, ILLINOIS 14

In a game between teams with losing records and in which 6-foot-1, 196-pound Ron Johnson was expected to set a Michigan single-season rushing record — he picked up 61 yards and reached 876, eight short of Tom Harmon's record — it was 5-10, 169-pound defensive back George Hoey who delivered the key play. The Illini kicked to the junior from Flint, Michigan, who was leading the Big Ten in punt return average, just once in Champaign, and it was a doozy: Hoey grabbed the ball at Michigan's 40, sidestepped a pair of tacklers and sprinted to the end zone for a score that — after a two-point conversion — knotted the game at 14 in the third quarter. "After the first block I saw I was pretty clear," Hoey told the *Free Press*. "There was another block near the goal line. I thought it might be a clip, but it wasn't. I just saw daylight and kept running." A few minutes later, following an interception, Johnson pounded the ball in from three yards out for the winning score.

600
OCT. 21, 1978
U-M 42, WISCONSIN 0

The ninth-ranked Wolverines improved to 8-0 against Wisconsin since Bo Schembechler became coach in 1969 and 13-1-1 at Madison in a rout that showcased their mighty option-run game. U-M rushed 65 times for 360 yards against the Badgers — despite starting five of its six first-half posses-sions within 10 yards of midfield. Quarterback Rick Leach led the attack with 82 yards (on 12 carries), a 44-yard zigzag and two TDs on the ground; he also threw one TD pass — a 65-yard bomb to Ralph Clayton — while completing four passes for 101 yards (in seven attempts, including another long incompletion to Clayton). It was enough for Wisconsin coach Dave McClain: "Rick Leach is everything I thought he was. He's a great leader. He makes the great reads. That's what makes him so darn good with his options." With 200 completions in his career, Leach, a senior from Flint Southwestern, tied Don Moorhead's school record, set in 1970.

700
NOV. 4, 1989
U-M 42, PURDUE 27

History was made at the Big House, though not in the way the 105,128 folks in attendance might have expected from a 6-1 U-M squad facing the 1-6 Boilermakers. Purdue freshman Eric Hunter, in his first start, became the first player to pass for four TDs against Michigan, though three of them came after the fourth-ranked Wolverines had taken a 35-7 lead late in the third quarter. That gave Schembechler, in his final season, a chance to use it as a motivational tool: "I never thought we wouldn't win. But I don't like the looks of it. ... It was a wild game. That's all I can say about it. It was a wild game." Hunter completed 27 of 42 passes for 344 yards with two intercep-tions and two fumbles. "He's wild," Schembechler said. The Wolverines had two punts blocked, absorbed four sacks and were flagged for not having enough players on the line for a kickoff, drawing a headphones throw on the sideline from Schembechler. Still, the final score pacified him enough to joke about the 700th victory: "Fielding Yost is turning over in his grave and saying, 'Bo, what are you doing?' I'm sure he did. And I apologize, Fielding."

DAVID P. GILKEY/DETROIT FREE PRESS

As Ron Bellamy (No. 19) started to signal touchdown, wide receiver David Terrell showed off the proof that he scored the go-ahead points against 17th-ranked Wisconsin.

800
SEPT. 30, 2000
U-M 13, WISCONSIN 10

After 2½ seasons of hype — including two seasons of job-sharing with Tom Brady and a broken foot that delayed his junior year — Drew Henson made his first career start for the ninth-ranked Wolverines. Henson, who left Brighton High with the second-most passing yards and touchdowns in Michigan prep history, completed 15 of 27 passes for 257 yards — the most important of which came on a sky-high throw to David Terrell in the end zone with 6:42 left and U-M trailing the No. 17 Badgers by four. Terrell skied over two defenders (and teammate Ron Bellamy) to haul in the TD (one of five catches for 96 yards). The U-M defense, missing four starters, con-tained running back Michael Bennett for most of the day (holding the Big Ten sprint champ 114 yards under his 237-yard average) and recorded a fumble recovery and three inter-ceptions. It was certainly a learning experience for Henson, who lost two fumbles and was sacked three times. "The only difference is I am not used to playing for four quarters and being intense for three or 3½ hours," he said. Coach Lloyd Carr concluded: "He's got the right stuff, I'll tell you that."

809

OCT. 6, 2001
U-M 20, PENN STATE 0

The 15th-ranked Wolverines raised plenty of eyebrows with their shutout: It was the first time a Joe Paterno-coached team had been blanked at home. It was the first 0-4 start in Penn State history. It was the first time the Nittany Lions had lost three straight home games in the same season since 1964, two years before Paterno took the helm. It was the first time an opponent had won three straight at Penn State since Army in 1957, '61 and '63. It was Penn State's fifth straight loss to Michigan. It kept Paterno from tying Bear Bryant's major-college record of 323 victories. All that said, hardly anybody noticed that Michigan also passed Yale for the most victories in college football history. Coming into the season, the Bulldogs led U-M, 806-805. U-M won its opener Sept. 1 against Miami (Ohio) but lost at Washington on Sept. 8. Yale's opener, scheduled for Sept. 15, was canceled because of the 9/11 terrorist attacks. U-M's games slated for Sept. 15 (against Western Michigan) and Sept. 22 (against Illinois) were pushed back a week. U-M won 'em both while Yale beat Cornell and Holy Cross. As the calendar flipped to October, the teams remained tied at 808 victories. On Oct. 6, U-M held Penn State to 25 rushing yards on 26 carries, intercepted two passes and recovered a fumble. John Navarre completed 17 of 31 passes for 246 yards and two touchdowns, and B.J. Askew rushed 27 times for 122 yards. Yale didn't play until the next afternoon, which capped its 300th anniversary weekend on campus. The Bulldogs trailed Dartmouth, 32-20, with 7:09 left, but they marched 80 yards for a touchdown, got the ball back and reached the 12-yard line. Three straight incompletions resulted in a 32-27 loss to the Big Green and a 809-808 deficit to Big Blue. Soon after, U-M athletic director Bill Martin told the *Michigan Daily*: "If there's one thing I love about Michigan athletics, I think it's tradition — long-time tradition. I think this is an indication of that."

900

OCT. 20, 2012
U-M 12, MICHIGAN STATE 10

Forgive Michigan if victory No. 900 wasn't on the forefront of its collective mind in preparing for its instate rival. As coach Brady Hoke said afterward, "I'll be honest with you, I don't know if (the team) realized it was the 900th win. That wasn't the point of focus for the week." Indeed, the Wolverines were much more focused on taking back the Paul Bunyan Trophy after four straight MSU triumphs in the series. Victory No. 900 — the 68th over MSU — wasn't pretty: The 23rd-ranked Wolverines had nearly as many punts (seven) as points (nine) in the first 59:55. But in the final three minutes, U-M forced a three-and-out to get the ball back, drove 41 yards (thanks to a clutch 20-yard catch by Drew Dileo) and set up Brendan Gibbons' 38-yard field goal with five seconds left (with Dileo as the holder). Afterward, the Wolverines celebrated with Paul in the Big House. "I ran over there, and this is my first time beating Michigan State, so I don't know how that works, so I ran over there to get the Paul Bunyan Trophy because I remember that's how they did it," offensive tackle Taylor Lewan recounted of his search of MSU's sideline. "I didn't see it, so Coach Hoke told us to go sing The Victors, so I did that." Eventually, the trophy was delivered to the U-M locker room, and MSU claimed there was no hanky-panky. U-M fans stormed the field, prompting the MSU band to give up on its planned postgame performance.

KIRTHMON F. DOZIER/DETROIT FREE PRESS

With a hand from Cameron Gordon, Michigan's Brendan Gibbons got a little air after his 38-yard game-winning field goal with five seconds left. After four straight losses to Michigan State, the Wolverines finally could exhale.

After 144 seasons and 999 victories, the big one had finally arrived ... with a little help from the Wolverines' defense.

BRAD MILLS/USA TODAY SPORTS

Kenneth Grant delivered a 339-pound crushing blow to Maryland's Taulia Tagovailoa and the Terrapins' upset dreams. Grant's late sack pushed the Terps' back to their 2 for a third-and-18 and forced them to use a timeout. Then Mike Sainristil picked off a pass.

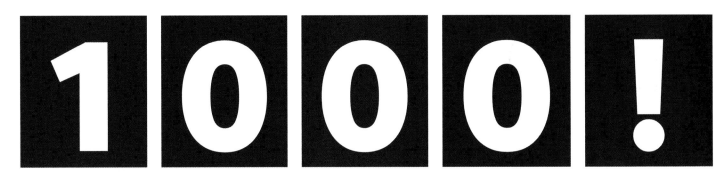

1000!

By Gene Myers
THE BIG PICTURE

Up 20 points midway through the second quarter, Michigan appeared to be cruising to another blowout, an 11-0 record in back-to-back seasons for the first time since 1901-02, its 1,000th all-time victory and, the following week, a battle of unbeatens in The Game.

But before a large contingent of Michigan fans stormed the field at SECU Stadium, before the team posed at midfield with giant "1000" signs and before every Blue thought could turn to a top-five showdown with Ohio State, the Wolverines were forced to scratch and claw like never before during their season of dominance.

Two outstanding plays came out of a first-quarter blocked punt. Christian Boivin laid out perfectly for Michigan's first block of the season. Maryland punter Brenden Segovia booted the bouncing ball out of the end zone to prevent a Michigan touchdown. The safety was U-M's first since December 2018 against Florida at the Peach Bowl and gave the Wolverines a 16-3 lead.

On its last three possessions, Maryland would have taken the lead with a touchdown. On its other two second-half possessions, Maryland scored touchdowns.

The defense, though, made big plays from start to finish. And then U-M won a game of inches in the closing minutes.

"Our motto I would say all year has been don't flinch," said nickelback Mike Sainristil, who made two interceptions. "That's with everything that's been going on within the program. Don't flinch, don't let anything affect you. Things aren't always going to go your way, just fall back on your technique, fall back on your details and keep fighting."

After Maryland kicked an early field goal, Michigan scored 23 straight points in less than 10 minutes. Blake Corum scored on a two-yard run, Maryland native Derrick Moore had a four-yard scoop-and-score fumble return, Christian Boivin blocked a punt for a safety and Corum scored on a one-yard run.

Maryland touchdowns on quarterback sneaks late in the first half and on its first possession of the second made it a game at 23-17. In between, J.J. McCarthy threw an interception at the goal line with 11 seconds until halftime. It was his first interception since Week 3. He seemed off all day, hobbled around a bit and had another pedestrian stat line, passing 12 of 23 for 141 yards, with no TDs for the third straight game. His rushing statistics: two attempts for minus-seven yards.

After Sainristil's first interception, freshman Semaj Morgan scored on a 13-yard end-around. But Maryland hustled 84 yards in nine plays, scored on its third one-yard sneak by backup QB Billy Edwards Jr. and trailed only 29-24 entering the fourth quarter.

Maryland's three fourth-quarter possessions consisted of 11 plays that lost 11 yards. The possessions ended with a punt (after a Mason Graham sack), an interception (Sainristil's second) and a safety (intentional grounding by Taulia Tagovailoa in the end zone).

The safety was set up by Tommy Doman's 47-yard punt that bounced once toward the goal line only to bounce again but backward; Caden Kolesar downed the ball inside the 1. After the safety, only the center, the quarterback and the tailback touched the ball for Michigan. Corum, who ran six straight times on the possession, converted a fourth-and-one from the Terrapins' 38 with 1:53 left to play. It was close but upheld by video review.

After posing for posterity on the opponents' turf, the Wolverines thought of Jim Harbaugh, their suspended coach, and That School Down South, the second-ranked Ohio State Buckeyes.

"There's no doubt in my mind that when we head back to the airport, he's going to be there waiting for us," Sainristil said of Harbaugh. "We'll probably take 10 to 15 minutes to take another picture at the airplane with him, just to be able to celebrate and cherish this moment."

Acting head coach Sherrone Moore had a different strategy: "We need to edit Coach in there. There's enough technology in the world today that we can get that done."

And more to do in the regular-season finale.

"We all know what time it is," sixth-year linebacker Mike Barrett said. "Once this game was over, we knew where our attention was going to go."

THE PREAMBLE

▶▶ Jim Harbaugh's first public comments about his latest suspension came at his weekly Monday news conference. He didn't get into any specifics, instead thanking everyone in Blue from president Santa Ono to the fan base for their support. He said he looked forward to a Friday hearing in U-M's attempt for a temporary restraining order against the Big Ten's punishment. He also said he always wanted to be a lawyer and referenced one of his favorite TV shows, Judge Judy, and the Tom Cruise/Jack Nicholson courtroom drama movie, A Few Good Men.

▶▶ A day before the scheduled hearing, U-M dropped its pursuit of a restraining order. Michigan announced in a statement that the Big Ten "agreed to close its investigation" and that U-M and Harbaugh "agreed to accept the three-game suspension." In its statement, the conference said U-M was "a valued member of the Big Ten" and the conference would "continue to work cooperatively with the university and the NCAA during this process."

▶▶ The next day, linebackers coach Chris Partridge was fired. Who did the firing? A spokesman would only say, "Michigan Athletics." Why was Partridge fired? "Consistent with our commitment to integrity," associate AD Kurt Svoboda said, "we will continue to cooperate with the NCAA as it moves forward with its ongoing investigation, including disciplinary measures, based on information we obtain." Picked to handle Partridge's duties was Rick Minter, a former head coach at Cincinnati, a defensive analyst at U-M and the father of defensive coordinator Jesse Minter.

▶▶ As 19½-point favorites against Maryland, the Wolverines were positioned to win their 1,000th game in 144 years of football. The Terrapins entered the game 6-4 overall and 3-4 in the Big Ten and 0-33 against ranked Big Ten opponents since joining the conference in 2014.

BRAD MILLS/USA TODAY SPORTS

Less than five minutes into the third quarter, Maryland had trimmed a 20-point U-M lead to 23-17. Six minutes later, Semaj Morgan restored a two-possession lead with a scintillating 13-yard reverse.

BRAD MILLS/USA TODAY SPORTS

Edge rusher Jaylen Harrell chased down Taulia Tagovailoa in the first quarter for the second of five Michigan sacks. They resulted in 53 yards in losses for the Terrapins.

THE PLAY-BY-PLAY

▶▶ Passing 21 of 31 for 247 yards, Taulia Tagovailoa — the most dangerous quarterback U-M had faced — threw for more yards than any other opposing QB to that point in the season. But Tagovailoa, whose brother Tua was a Heisman Trophy runner-up with Alabama, was sacked five times, threw two interceptions and lost a fumble.

▶▶ The Terrapins gained 71 yards on the ground, but lost 53 yards on the five sacks and two yards on two tackles for a loss and one yard on a kneel-down. Their 15 net yards averaged out to 0.5 yards a carry on 33 rushes.

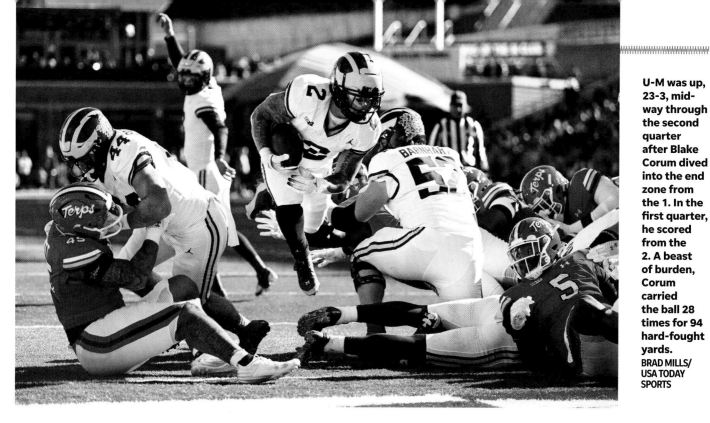

U-M was up, 23-3, midway through the second quarter after Blake Corum dived into the end zone from the 1. In the first quarter, he scored from the 2. A beast of burden, Corum carried the ball 28 times for 94 hard-fought yards.
BRAD MILLS/ USA TODAY SPORTS

THE PRESS BOX

▶▶▶ **RAINER SABIN, DETROIT FREE PRESS:** "The final throw J.J. McCarthy unleashed in the first half was intercepted, ending a promising drive that took the Wolverines to the cusp of the end zone. It offered a painful reminder of that famous Darrell Royal quote — also attributed to Woody Hayes — 'Three things can happen when you pass the ball, and two of them are bad.' Late in the season, during its most crucial stretch, it seems as if Michigan has come to the same conclusion. The Wolverines have reverted to a ground-based attack after leaning on McCarthy's arm during the first nine games."

▶▶▶ **SHAWN WINDSOR, DETROIT FREE PRESS:** "For the third game in a row, for the sixth time this fall, Harbaugh won't be on the sidelines next week. Some players will feel his absence more than others. No one will feel it quite like McCarthy. To get through Ohio State, he'll have to find the same kind of comfort and spark without him."

THE PRIME NUMBER
8TH
Place on Michigan's career passing yardage list for J.J. McCarthy after his 141-yard day. With 5,570 yards, he moved ahead of his coach, Jim Harbaugh, who had 5,449 yards from 1983-86.

BRAD MILLS/USA TODAY SPORTS

With Jim Harbaugh on the sideline, J.J. McCarthy had thrown 11 TD passes and no interceptions. Without him, McCarthy had seven TDs and four picks.

THE PROCLAMATIONS

▶▶▶ **TAILBACK BLAKE CORUM:** "Maybe we needed this test a little bit. Maybe we needed a close game like this — not saying Penn State wasn't close — but they gave us more for our money out there."

▶▶▶ **MARYLAND COACH MIKE LOCKSLEY:** "I'm not up here to celebrate a moral victory at all. ... To have a breakthrough win, our team played the script to a tee except to finish."

THE POLLS

▶▶▶ The fourth edition of the College Football Playoff rankings saw Washington pass Florida State for the all-important fourth spot. That happened because the Huskies beat highly regarded Oregon State, 22-20, and the Seminoles fell behind North Alabama, 13-0, and lost quarterback Jordan Travis to a gruesome broken leg before storming to a 58-13 victory. The CFP's top five were the only unbeaten Power Five teams. The next three CFP teams had one loss (Oregon, Texas, Alabama).

RK	TEAM	W-L	PVS
1.	Georgia	11-0	2
2.	Ohio State	11-0	1
3.	Michigan	11-0	3
4.	Washington	11-0	5
5.	Florida State	11-0	4

▶▶▶ Ohio State and Michigan traded places — OSU up to No. 2, U-M down to No. 3 — in the US LBM coaches and the AP media polls. The AP top 10: Georgia, OSU, Michigan, Washington, FSU, Oregon, Texas, Alabama, Louisville, Missouri.

The Wolverines iced the Buckeyes with a rare hat trick: Three straight series wins, and three straight East titles.

JUNFU HAN/DETROIT FREE PRESS

On the first play after Zak Zinter was carted off with a gruesome leg injury, with the game tied at 17, Blake Corum broke past the line, shook off an arm tackle and motored 22 yards into the end zone. Before that, he had rushed 12 times for 28 yards.

Blue streak!

By Mitch Albom

THE BIG PICTURE

Thrillers aren't thrillers until the hero gets in trouble.

And everything that happened until the third quarter in the Big House thriller, when Zak Zinter went down with a leg injury so gruesome Fox wouldn't show the replay, was just buildup.

Zak Zinter's All-America season ended late in the third quarter when he suffered a broken tibia and fibula in his left leg. As he was being carted off, the Big House provided a rousing ovation. He extended his left arm and the cheering grew louder.
JUNFU HAN/ DETROIT FREE PRESS

After that — after the entire Michigan team gathered around their senior captain and best offensive lineman, after Zinter was rolled off in a medical cart, after he shook a fist at the crowd and Michigan Stadium roared with approval — suddenly we were inside something bigger than a football game, something even people who never have made a tackle could relate to.

"I looked back and Zak was screaming and Karsen (Barnhart) was literally holding his foot (because) it was just limp; it was a sight I don't wish upon anyone," quarterback J.J. McCarthy said. "At that moment, seeing that look in everybody's eyes, seeing them rally together, (there) was something about it. It was spiritual, honestly. It was a different drive ... after that happened."

He was right. As if maize-and-blue pixie dust had dropped from the late autumn sky, tailback Blake Corum, who referred to Zinter as "my

guy," took a handoff on the very next play and, despite having been bottled up all day, burst outside, escaped a tackle and raced 22 yards to the corner of the end zone.

He held up six fingers then five fingers, for the No. 65 that Zinter wore. But he could just have easily held up a "V" for victory.

Or vindication.

In one of the finest of Big Games in the 119 years of this Michigan-Ohio State rivalry — and one of the most intense — the Wolverines remained undefeated, winning 30-24 and flooding the field with a sea of delirious fans. For the third straight year, Michigan sent Buckeyes coach Ryan Day home with his head hanging as low as a man walking to his execution.

"Devastating," he called it. And in Columbus, they used harsher words. U-M won because it made fewer mistakes, ran the ball better, played the clock brilliantly, converted gutsy fourth downs

and stabbed the crimson bull every time it threatened to charge.

But mostly it won on heart — and timing. Ohio State may have had the flashy talent, but Michigan had the brightest moments, be it an early interception that led to a touchdown, a made-you-blink threaded TD by McCarthy to Roman Wilson between two defenders ("Insane!" Wilson later called that pass) or the cherry-on-the-top moment in the final 25 seconds. That's when Ohio State's Kyle McCord, directing a desperate drive for a winning score, was pressured by Jaylen Harrell. McCord tried slinging a pass to star receiver Marvin Harrison Jr. but saw it flutter into the arms of a diving Rod Moore for a game-sealing interception.

Moore, who grew up in Ohio and came to Michigan after the Buckeyes didn't offer him a scholarship, couldn't believe what he had accomplished. "I really can't put it

in words how I'm feeling," he said. "I was on the field looking like, 'I just called game.' I did that!"

He sure did. A kid who was told by friends when he enrolled at Ann Arbor that he would never beat Ohio State now had done it three years in a row.

You know what they call that? Vindication.

And that, of course, must be the theme of this victory. If you believe in punishment, then you must believe in retribution. For the third straight week, the Wolverines played without their coach, Jim Harbaugh. It was the most difficult stretch of their season — on the road against No. 10 Penn State, on the road against Maryland and at home against No. 2 Ohio State — a tripleheader that rivaled almost any school's three-game stretch this season.

The Wolverines won all three. Without Harbaugh. And certainly without any pregame sign stealing. Acting

head coach Sherrone Moore was asked whether the victory put to rest the idea that somehow Michigan wasn't really as good as it seemed due to an unfair advantage.

"There are a lot of things I would love to say," he answered cryptically. "All I know is this team is as good as any team in the country. And I think they just prove it every week."

They proved it on a sunny, 35-degree afternoon by staying just out of reach of the Buckeyes' powerful attack, like a man protected by a shark cage. Although Michigan's defense stymied Ohio State early on, the second half saw OSU rev it up, with running back TreVeyon Henderson chugging yardage and Harrison proving nearly unstoppable if the ball was thrown anywhere near him.

Michigan's 14-3 first-half lead was erased in the third quarter, and the Buckeyes tied the game at 17 with 5:35 left in the period. If you had paused the game at that moment, you likely would have put money on Harrison, Henderson and the OSU defense to emerge victorious. They certainly seemed to have the momentum.

But football, like life, is a pendulum of emotions, and when Zinter went down and the entire team watched him lifted onto that medical cart (the image of massive 322-pound linemen looking teary-eyed speaks volumes about the dangers of this game), the pendulum swung the other way.

And when Corum ripped off that 22-yard run on the next play, then flashed the "65" for the cameras, you almost could hear him and his team declaring, "We are not losing this game."

From that point on, the volume boomed, the gas pedal was slammed. The game took on a storm-like intensity, as if set against a backdrop of blinding lightning and rolling thunder. Every hit mattered. Every first down was gold.

"No one cried, no one whined, we were just like, 'OK, if this is what we have to do, this is what we have to do,'" Corum said. "The job has to get done no matter what

THE PREAMBLE

▶▶▶ Win and play for a third straight Big Ten championship, a third consecutive trip to the College Football Playoff and a shot at the first national championship in 26 years. Lose and end up in a nice enough bowl in a nice enough city but with a shell of the team because the NFL-bound players would sit out. It was that simple: Win or bust. The Wolverines were favored by 3½ points.

▶▶▶ As much as the Wolverines and Buckeyes disliked each other — and the feud between Jim Harbaugh and Ryan Day had been well-documented for years — material for the opposing bulletin board was tough to find. At his weekly news conference, Harbaugh dodged a question about Day but addressed all the "noise" — allegations, suspensions, firings and vitriol — by delivering a deadpan joke from Ted Lasso: "I'm just so proud, so proud of our team. Despite that noise, our locker room's in one piece. Like Ted, for me, locker rooms (are) a lot like my mom's bathing suits. I like to see them in one piece."

▶▶▶ Updates on the sign-stealing front: Yahoo! Sports reported that the NCAA notified the Big Ten that there were no known ties between Day or his family and the investigation. Yahoo also reported that an unnamed booster known as Uncle T may have at least partially funded the sign-stealing operation (and the booster wasn't Tom Brady). And the *Free Press*, after an open-records request, discovered that Connor Stalions never filed a single expense report during his employment at U-M.

JUNFU HAN/DETROIT FREE PRESS

Michigan fans screamed like banshees during the battle of unbeatens. With 110,615 people at the Big House, it was the 315th straight crowd in excess of 100,000 (except for a few COVID-19 games in 2020) at Michigan Stadium.

JUNFU HAN/DETROIT FREE PRESS

A former offensive lineman at Oklahoma, Sherrone Moore truly had become a big man on campus. His resume: 4-0, top-10 W's over Ohio State and Penn State.

— whether Coach is here, whether players are hurt. The job has to get done and the job will get done. ...

"It's been great. A little adversity, feeling like everyone's against you, Michigan versus everybody. ... It's been nothing but great."

Vindicated.

Somebody shooting one of those Heisman Trophy commercials? Charles Woodson (right), the 1997 winner, chatted with Desmond Howard, the 1991 winner, on the sideline during the game. Michigan's other Heisman winner was Tom Harmon in 1940.
JUNFU HAN/DETROIT FREE PRESS

For the first time since the MSU game, J.J. McCarthy and Roman Wilson hooked up for a touchdown pass. Wilson's 11th TD catch of the season — a 22-yarder — built Michigan's lead to 14-3 with 10:22 left in the first half. Wilson finished with three catches for 36 yards.

THE PLAY-BY-PLAY

▶▶▶ On the game's first scoring drive, after a Will Johnson interception put the ball at the OSU 7, the Buckeyes stopped Blake Corum on third-and-goal from the 1 but not fourth-and-goal from the 1. It was the first of three successful fourth-down conversions for U-M.

▶▶▶ The Wolverines kept the ball for 10:28 in the final quarter, their two drives leading to medium-range field goals by James Turner. The first drive included a deep pass from Donovan Edwards to Colston Loveland for 34 yards. The second drive lasted 13 plays, took seven minutes and forced OSU to use its three timeouts.

▶▶▶ For the 22nd straight meeting, the winning team outrushed the losing team. U-M gained 156 yards on the ground to OSU's 107.

▶▶▶ OSU's Marvin Harrison Jr., later a Heisman Trophy finalist, caught five passes for 118 yards, with a 44-yard gain and a 14-yard touchdown. Harrison and QB Kyle McCord failed to connect on four other targets. Corum led all rushers with 88 yards on 22 carries and two TDs. His 22 rushing scores for the season broke Hassan Haskins' U-M record of 20 set in 2021. Loveland caught five passes for 88 yards.

Blake Corum and his backfield friends scratched and clawed for every inch against the stout Buckeyes. Michigan averaged 4.0 yards for its 39 carries. "We're battle tested," Corum said.

Ohio State coach Ryan Day got an escort off the field. He should have been more worried about his reception back home. ADAM CAIRNS/USA TODAY SPORTS

THE PRIME NUMBER

3

Number of losses to Big Ten opponents in Ryan Day's five-plus seasons leading Ohio State — all to Michigan. He won the other 41 games for a .932 winning percentage.

THE POLLS

▶▶▶ The next-to-last edition of the College Football Playoff rankings saw Ohio State tumbled from second to sixth after its 30-24 loss to the Wolverines. Michigan, Washington and Florida State moved up one place. Four one-loss teams remained in contention: Oregon, Texas, Alabama and Ohio State. The Buckeyes were the longest shot because they didn't reach a conference championship game. The title matchups: No. 1 Georgia vs. No. 8 Alabama, No. 2 Michigan vs. No. 16 Iowa, No. 3 Washington vs. No. 5 Oregon, No. 4 FSU vs. No. 14 Louisville, No. 7 Texas vs. No. 18 Oklahoma State.

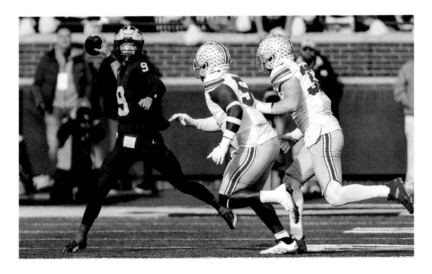

J.J. McCarthy threw for 148 yards (16 of 20) and one TD. "Coach Moore said from the get-go that he's going to call the most aggressive game he's ever called," McCarthy said. "That's music to our ears." JUNFU HAN/ DETROIT FREE PRESS

RK	TEAM	W-L	PVS
1.	Georgia	12-0	1
2.	Michigan	12-0	3
3.	Washington	12-0	4
4.	Florida State	12-0	5
5.	Oregon	11-1	6

▶▶▶ The top 10 in the US LBM coaches poll and the AP media poll were identical: Georgia, Michigan, Washington, FSU, Oregon, OSU, Texas, Alabama, Missouri, Penn State.

THE PROCLAMATIONS

▶▶▶ **TAILBACK BLAKE CORUM:** "My last four years, I look back and pray I left a legacy. I stamped my mark here, I made a difference, on and off the field. You know, looking back at this game, I feel like this is why I came back. I couldn't go out at the Big House like I did last year, hurt. I came back for a game like this."

▶▶▶ **OHIO STATE COACH RYAN DAY:** "There's a locker room in there that's devastated. It wasn't a lack of effort, but again, we didn't win the rushing yards, we didn't win the turnover battle. So you're not going to win this game."

THE PRESS BOX

▶▶▶ **JEFF SEIDEL, DETROIT FREE PRESS:** "Sherrone Moore deserves credit, too. This young, talented coach just outdueled Ryan Day — all day long. Whenever Harbaugh decides to leave Michigan, his replacement is pretty dang obvious."

▶▶▶ **SHAWN WINDSOR, DETROIT FREE PRESS:** "The most notable difference between this year's team and the last two — beyond McCarthy's first-round skill set and the experience he has in using it — remains on the defensive side of the ball. U-M's D-line is big, fast, versatile and relentless. Its linebackers run like safeties."

THE SEASON 99

3

THE CHAMPS

Winning the Big Ten was just the start. Next came the battle for the Roses against college football royalty in Alabama. And then, finally, a Texas two-step with a familiar foe from out West.

He who wanted a rose must respect the thorn, right? With captains like Blake Corum, the Wolverines earned their roses in Pasadena in part thanks to their ignoring of all the thorny issues.
JUNFU HAN/DETROIT FREE PRESS

KIRTHMON F. DOZIER/DETROIT FREE PRESS

At Jim Harbaugh's request, Big Ten commissioner Tony Petitti handed the Stagg Trophy not to him as coach of the Big Ten champions but to Zak Zinter, Michigan's All-America guard who suffered a horrific leg injury against Ohio State. Crutches nearby, Zinter was more than happy to accept the silver football and share the moment with teammates such as Mike Sainristil (No. 0) and Josaiah Stewart (No. 5).

Another trip to Indy brought a familiar result: The Big Ten title — and a chance to play for even more.

KIRTHMON F. DOZIER/DETROIT FREE PRESS

Freshman Semaj Morgan electrified the Michigan fans at Lucas Oil Stadium with an 87-yard punt return to the Iowa 5 late in the first quarter.

Triple play

By Tony Garcia
THE BIG PICTURE

The night seemed like a formality from the beginning. At no point was there any doubt in the outcome.

The real drama in the Big Ten championship game figured to come during the presentation of the Stagg Trophy, when tradition called for the newbie Big Ten commissioner, Tony Petitti, to hand off the silver football to the ol' quarterback, Jim Harbaugh.

JUNFU HAN/DETROIT FREE PRESS

Junior tailback Donovan Edwards, the MVP of the 2022 championship game, celebrated another title by doing confetti angels.

When Michigan freshman Semaj Morgan set a title game record with an 87-yard punt return to the Iowa 5 late in the first quarter and Blake Corum was in the end zone two plays later, Lucas Oil Stadium felt more like Ann Arbor South than the league's centrally located indoor stadium.

But the reality really set in early in the third quarter when Mike Sainristil forced his second fumble of the game, setting up the Wolverines with a first-and-goal at the Iowa 6 and ensuring he would be the game's MVP. Corum immediately plowed his way into the end zone again — his 55th rushing touchdown, tying Anthony Thomas' career record at U-M.

With 24 minutes left to play, the Wolverines owned a 17-0 lead that felt like 170-0. The Hawkeyes had run 29 plays, gained 67 yards and made two first downs. After eight possessions, they had lost two fumbles, endured

four three-and-outs and punted two other times.

Three James Turner field goals put the finishing touches on a 26-0 victory, only the second shutout in title game history.

"I've been trying to grasp it because I've been watching on TV the last two years and I'm finally in it, so it feels real to me," Morgan said. "I've been telling people my whole college journey these, just this whole 10 months, 11 months, it feels like a dream to me.

"The team I'm on, the coaches I'm around, everybody that supports us. Feels like a dream, like a movie."

For the first time in its 144 years of football, the Wolverines captured three consecutive outright Big Ten titles. While beating Iowa in 2021, Purdue in 2022 and Iowa again, Michigan surrendered only nine second-half points. And none of those were scored by the Hawkeyes.

As ugly as it was for Iowa,

its stout defense made the game a slog for the Wolverines. U-M put together a simple, yet effective (enough) game plan. J.J. McCarthy completed 22 of 30 passes for 147 yards and no completion longer than 14 yards. He lost 40 yards on four sacks. Corum needed 16 rushes to grind out 52 yards, no run longer than his six-yard TD effort.

U-M's 213 yards (147 passing, 66 rushing) marked its lowest total of the season by 74 yards (287 against Penn State).

"Today's performance, it wasn't our best," Corum said, "but there's nothing better than winning. It got the job done."

The defense was the star of the day. The unit forced as many punts as it allowed first downs (seven apiece). It forced three turnovers. It kept Iowa from converting three times on fourth downs. It allowed its fewest yards of the season, a measly 155 yards on 120 passing and 35 rushing.

"Glorious defensive performance," Harbaugh said. "Just tremendous, lights-out. Three-and-outs. ... So just spectacular."

Besides his two forced fumbles, Sainristil registered a sack and broke up a pass. The only other defensive player to win the game's MVP was Michigan edge rusher and Heisman Trophy runner-up Aidan Hutchinson in 2021.

"Just a playmaker, when a play has to be made, when the magic needs to happen, Mike makes it happen," Harbaugh said. "It's been game after game. Especially down the stretch here these final four games, he has been a stalwart. He intercepts, makes the big hit, makes the big hit in the fumble, causes a fumble. Just an incredible player."

Harbaugh became the first coach to win three consecutive outright Big Ten titles.

"To me, it feels 10 out of 10 happy," he said. "Like it did last year, and like it did in '21."

Kris Jenkins shared a hug with Janet Snow, his grand-mother. KIRTHMON F.DOZIER/DFP

JUNFU HAN/*DETROIT FREE PRESS*

On a blitz at the Iowa 9, nickelback Mike Sainristil dislodged the ball from Deacon Hill's throwing hand, Josh Wallace recovered the fumble, Iowa OC Brian Ferentz received a penalty for unsportsmanlike conduct and, on the next play, Blake Corum scored on a six-yard run for a 17-0 U-M lead.

THE PLAY-BY-PLAY

▶▶▶ McNamara's replacement, Deacon Hill, looked more like a lineman than a quarterback at 6-feet-3 and 258 pounds. He entered the game completing 48.3 percent of his passes and with more interceptions than touchdowns. Hounded all night, Hill completed 18 of 32 passes for 120 yards. His longest completion covered 19 yards. He didn't throw an interception, but he lost two fumbles and was sacked four times.

▶▶▶ When Michigan's opening drive led to a 35-yard field goal by James Turner, it marked the first time all season Iowa had given up points on an opponent's first possession. Turner's fourth field of the game — a 50-yarder — was the longest ever in the championship game.

▶▶▶ Michigan's linebacking corps led the team in tackles: eight apiece for Junior Colson and Ernest Hausmann and seven for Michael Barrett.

THE PREAMBLE

▶▶▶ Jim Harbaugh was fired up on a Sunday conference call to preview the Big Ten championship game. The victory over Ohio State? "Probably the happiest I've ever been. One of the happiest moments of my life." The road ahead? "I know I talk about 'the team, the team, the team.' To me, this is the team. The '23 team. It's the team."

▶▶▶ Although 10-2 and ranked 16th, Iowa remained a team of polar opposites. Led by Phil Parker, soon to win the Broyles Award as the country's top assistant coach, Iowa's defense ranked among the best: No. 4 in scoring (12.2 points), No. 5 in total yards (279.3), No. 9 against the pass (174.3) and No. 15 against the run (104.9). Led by Brian Ferentz, already told he would be fired after the season, Iowa's offense ranked among the country's worst: No. 120 in scoring (18.0), No. 133 (dead last) in total yards (247.3), No. 130 passing (123.4) and No. 101 running (123.9).

▶▶▶ Plus, Iowa posted its anemic offensive numbers despite playing half its games against mediocre-at-best West Division opponents. The Hawkeyes would have to face a Michigan defense whose bona fides were off the charts: No. 1 in scoring (10.3), No. 2 in total yards (247.4), No. 2 against the pass (155.3) and No. 8 against the run (92.1).

▶▶▶ But did the Hawkeyes have a secret weapon in quarterback Cade McNamara? The former U-M captain entered the transfer portal right before the 2022 championship game. Iowa's offense really cratered after McNamara suffered a torn ACL in late September. "I know so much about that other team — from a defensive standpoint, from an offensive standpoint," he said. "I'm just doing everything I possibly can ... to just let these guys know everything that I possibly know."

▶▶▶ Iowa's game plan never varied: Play great defense, dominate special teams, capitalize on turnovers, display grit and heart. Its fans made signs with slogans like "Punting Is Winning." Still, the Wolverines were 21½-point favorites.

JUNFU HAN/DETROIT FREE PRESS

For the 55th time in his four years at Michigan, Blake Corum scored a rushing TD, tying Anthony Thomas atop U-M's career list. Corum had two TDs in 2020, 11 in 2021, 18 in 2022 and 24 thus far in 2023.

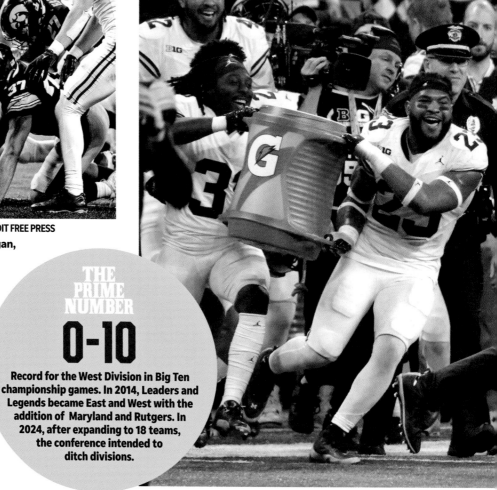

THE PROCLAMATIONS

▶▶▶ **COACH JIM HARBAUGH:**
"Incredible feeling. What our team planned for, hoped for, worked for."

▶▶▶ **TAILBACK BLAKE CORUM:** "We have a month now. A month to get guys healthy. We have a month to watch a lot of film. We have a month to practice a lot. We have time. We can't waste our time, but we have time."

▶▶▶ **NICKELBACK MIKE SAINRISTIL:** "Blake just said it: The narrative has changed. But for some odd reason, people look at Michigan, (and) they'll say we don't play whoever, we don't deserve to be wherever we are. But as we say, the only things that matter is what happens inside Schembechler Hall."

THE PRESS BOX

▶▶▶ **RAINER SABIN, DETROIT FREE PRESS:** "Go back to the summer of 2021 and Harbaugh stood inside this very same venue and declared his struggling program would either find a way to overtake Ohio State and win the league or 'die trying.' But 28 months after Harbaugh made that dramatic statement, so much has changed to the point that the latest coronation of the Wolverines as Big Ten kings has become anticlimactic."

▶▶▶ **SHAWN WINDSOR, DETROIT FREE PRESS:** "No team should ever apologize for earning confetti. Or for winning a game that ends with a makeshift stage on the field. Jim Harbaugh certainly won't. Nor should he."

THE PRIME NUMBER

0-10

Record for the West Division in Big Ten championship games. In 2014, Leaders and Legends became East and West with the addition of Maryland and Rutgers. In 2024, after expanding to 18 teams, the conference intended to ditch divisions.

CONFERENCE KINGS

With its 26-0 victory over Iowa, Michigan joined Ohio State as the only teams to win three straight Big Ten championship games. The history (all games played at Lucas Oil Stadium in Indianapolis and all MVPs from the winning team):

YEAR	RESULT	MVP
2011	Wisconsin 42, Michigan State 39	QB Russell Wilson
2012	Wisconsin 70, Nebraska 31	RB Montee Ball
2013	Michigan State 34, Ohio State 24	QB Connor Cook
2014	Ohio State 59, Wisconsin 0	QB Cardale Jones
2015	Michigan State 16, Iowa 13	QB Connor Cook
2016	Penn State 38, Wisconsin 31	QB Trace McSorley
2017	Ohio State 27, Wisconsin 21	RB J.K. Dobbins
2018	Ohio State 45, Northwestern 24	QB Dwayne Haskins
2019	Ohio State 34, Wisconsin 21	QB Justin Fields
2020	Ohio State 22, Northwestern 10	RB Trey Sermon
2021	Michigan 42, Iowa 3	DE Aidan Hutchinson
2022	Michigan 43, Purdue 22	RB Donovan Edwards
2023	Michigan 26, Iowa 0	DB Mike Sainristil

A scrambler from his playing days, Jim Harbaugh managed to elude a Gatorade bath from his players.
KIRTHMON F. DOZIER/DFP

THE POLLS

▶▶▶ Michigan rose to the top of the College Football Playoff rankings, the US LBM coaches poll and the AP media poll — its first time at No. 1 since the 1997 team shared the national championship with Nebraska. Georgia lost its place in the playoffs by losing to Alabama, 27-24. Florida State lost its place not by losing on the field but by failing the eye test after the season-ending injury to ace QB Jordan Travis. Washington beat Oregon for the second time by three points, 34-31. By blitzing Oklahoma State, 49-21, and owning a September victory over Alabama, Texas punched its ticket to the CFP tournament. Semifinal matchups: Michigan vs. Alabama, Washington vs. Texas.

RK	TEAM	W-L	PVS
1.	Michigan	13-0	2
2.	Washington	13-0	3
3.	Texas	12-1	7
4.	Alabama	12-1	8
5.	Florida State	13-0	4
6.	Georgia	12-1	1
7.	Ohio State	11-1	6
8.	Oregon	11-2	5
9.	Missouri	10-2	9
10.	Penn State	10-2	10

▶▶▶ The top 10 in the US LBM coaches poll: Michigan, Washington, FSU, Texas, Alabama, Georgia, OSU, Oregon, Missouri, PSU. The order for the AP media poll was identical except that Texas was third and FSU fourth.

THE POSTSCRIPT

▶▶▶ When the game mercifully ended, Jim Harbaugh scrambled along the sideline to avoid a Gatorade bath, a makeshift stage appeared on the field, and the real moment of truth arrived. How would Big Ten commissioner Tony Petitti and Harbaugh — distant adversaries for nearly two months — interact face-to-face during the presentation of the Stagg Trophy?

▶▶▶ Well, they didn't. Harbaugh pulled a rope-a-dope.

▶▶▶ The partisan Michigan crowd already had roundly booed Petitti, who didn't exactly stand front and center on the stage. Harbaugh stood even farther in the background, hugging and accepting congratulations.

▶▶▶ When Fox's Joel Klatt was cued to emcee the festivities (or fisticuffs?), he told the world: "To present tonight's championship trophy, Coach Harbaugh wanted it to go to Zak Zinter. So the commissioner of the Big Ten, Tony Petitti, the trophy, to 65, Zak Zinter."

▶▶▶ Among additional boos for Petitti, cheers rang out for Zinter, the senior captain and offensive lineman who suffered a broken leg against Ohio State.

▶▶▶ Awkward moment averted, Klatt eventually corralled Harbaugh and asked him how it felt to have won three straight Big Ten championships.

▶▶▶ Harbaugh shouted, "Bet!"

▶▶▶ He laughed, grinned and raised his right arm. Klatt cracked up. The players on stage went crazy.

▶▶▶ "We were waiting for that awkward moment," defensive end Kris Jenkins told the *Detroit News*. "For (Petitti), it was probably awkward, but for us, it was a little validating."

S-E-C YOU SOON

JUNFU HAN/DETROIT FREE PRESS

Been there, done that? Jim Harbaugh appeared a bit subdued and just taking in the scene soon after winning his third straight Big Ten title. He was fired up again a day later talking about his next opponent: "Two true blue bloods of college football, Michigan and Alabama."

Alabama's upset of Georgia and Florida State's ACC flop set up a showdown between the SEC and the Big Ten's best.

By Rainer Sabin

When the suspense was finally over and the last team selected for the College Football Playoff was announced, it felt as if a vacuum had sucked the air out the large banquet room on the Westin hotel's second floor.

An audible gasp was heard and then a hush fell over the expectant crowd of Michigan players mere minutes after they turned away from their buffet breakfast in Indianapolis to boisterously cheer the committee's decision to slot them No. 1.

JOHN DAVID MERCER/USA TODAY SPORTS

Nick Saban relished the feeling after vanquishing Kirby Smart and his two-time defending champion Georgia Bulldogs. As for the Wolverines? "What little I have seen is they're a great defensive team."

Their brief euphoria quickly had been supplanted by the sobering realization that the Wolverines had been matched against fourth-seeded Alabama in the Rose Bowl on New Year's Day.

The newly minted SEC champion might have pried its way into the exclusive tournament with Michigan, Washington and Texas after overcoming a bumpy start to its season. It might have shown the kinds of vulnerabilities rarely seen in the decorated squads the Crimson Tide had fielded in the past. But this was still Alabama, the powerhouse that had been the dominant program in this sport over the last 15 years. Six national titles during that span imbued Alabama with an enduring mystique and fear factor that already caused Michigan's sixth-year linebacker Michael Barrett to fret.

"My biggest concern about Alabama?" Barrett said. "Just the hype of the name, honestly. I just want all the guys to know it's a nameless, faceless opponent."

The muted response from Barrett's teammates after they learned they had drawn the Crimson Tide suggested his wish won't come easily.

Alabama had proven it could succeed in this four-team competition, where the Crimson Tide boasted a 6-1 record in the semifinal round. Michigan, on the other hand, had not. It failed to win each of the last two years in the CFP, further tarnishing the program's dismal postseason record that was besmirched with 29 losses in 50 bowls. Jim Harbaugh contributed the last six losses (against one victory). Because of that dodgy track record, there were reasonable questions about whether the Wolverines could succeed beyond the Big Ten, where they had won 25 straight games and claimed the past three titles.

Harbaugh implemented a "Beat Georgia" period in practice with the expectation that the Wolverines eventually would encounter the reigning champions of the past two years. But, in a strange twist, they instead meet Alabama, the progenitor of Kirby Smart's SEC behemoth and the team that snapped the mighty Bulldogs' 29-game winning streak in the SEC championship game, 27-24.

"It's iconic," Harbaugh said. "It's Alabama. It's 'Roll Tide.' ... It's gonna be competition. That's what this team lives for."

Harbaugh tried to convince a dubious audience of reporters that the Wolverines relished the prospect of facing Alabama and its legendary coach, Nick Saban. But it was a hard sell. Saban gave his program an advantage over the rest of the CFP field, which featured three teams with coaches who had never won a game in this tournament.

Alabama didn't boast its usual embarrassment of riches. But it had Saban and it still transmitted an ineffable aura that gave it a unique psychological edge.

Tailback Blake Corum, a proud Michigan Man, didn't buy that.

"We're not going to say that is Alabama, a team that has won, won, won, won," he said. "The committee chose us to being the No. 1 team. So, I'm not going to act like we're not."

The committee, which included U-M athletic director Warde Manuel, made safe picks putting Michigan and Washington at 1-2. But the committee raised a stink when it selected one-loss Texas and Alabama at 3-4 and bypassed Florida State, making the Seminoles the first unbeaten Power Five conference champion to be excluded from the field. A season-ending injury to quarterback Jordan Travis proved to be the deal-breaker.

"Florida State is a different team than they were through the first 11 weeks," said Boo Corrigan, the selection committee chairman and athletic director at North Carolina State, an ACC rival of FSU's.

Seminoles coach Mike Norvell blew a gasket: "I am disgusted and infuriated with the committee's decision today to have what was earned on the field taken away because a small group of people decided they knew better than the results of the games. What is the point of playing games? ... It's a sad day for college football."

To put Alabama in the field, the committee couldn't bypass the Longhorns, who beat the Tide, 34-24, at Tuscaloosa in September.

"It's unfortunate that some good team had to get left out," Saban said on ESPN, "but I really think that our team earned the right to be here."

So now the Crimson Tide was Michigan's problem.

"We've got to prove that we can hang with the best of them," defensive tackle Kris Jenkins said. "Right now, we've got a shot to play with the best of them."

Cutting, dashing, twisting, spinning and high-stepping, senior captain Blake Corum displayed all the skills in an All-America tailback's arsenal in a single 17-yard lightning bolt of a run that rocketed Michigan in front of Alabama in overtime at the Rose Bowl.

Just when it looked as if the Wolverines' time was up, they found another gear on offense ... and one last stop.

JUNFU HAN/DETROIT FREE PRESS

Defensive lineman Kris Jenkins, even at 305 pounds, displayed the quickest feet to lead the charge after Alabama's fourth-down failure.

A Rose above

By Rainer Sabin
THE BIG PICTURE

A s the sun set over the San Gabriel Mountains and light turned to darkness, the aperture of Michigan's season started to close and Alabama's grip over the Wolverines began to tighten.

The running lanes that were once there had narrowed. The passing windows that were available earlier in the game were closed. Then the lead the Wolverines held for more than 19 minutes vanished just like that.

Tommy Doman launched a second-half punt at the Rose Bowl, a venue described by Rainer Sabin of the *Free Press* as "the sport's most majestic stage, in its most picturesque setting." The Rose Bowl also was where many a great Michigan team went to fizzle.

When Jase McClellan coasted three yards into the end zone on the second play of the fourth quarter to help Alabama retake the lead at 17-13, the maize-and-blue crowd on the west side of the Rose Bowl shuddered.

It felt as if this was the beginning of the end in this College Football Playoff semifinal, when the Wolverines' dreams of a national championship would be dashed by Nick Saban's joyless murderball juggernaut on the sport's most majestic stage.

It seemed so cruel because only an hour or so before the same melancholy fans were buzzing with excitement. They had been invited to stand up and cheer by a pack of Michigan players who spent the first half delivering one body blow to Alabama after another. Matthew Hibner and Jimmy Rolder had just rocked Crimson Tide returner Kendrick Law on a kickoff. The thunderous hit reverberated moments after Tyler Morris snatched a pass from J.J. McCarthy, zipping up the sideline for a 38-yard touchdown that gave the Wolverines their first-ever lead in the College Football Playoff.

The euphoric sequence of events, which unfolded in a matter of seconds, tickled the imagination of Michigan supporters and offered definitive proof their favorite team finally belonged on this big stage. The Wolverines yearned for this opportunity ever since their stunning defeat to Texas

When season-long defensive hero Mike Sainristil failed to keep Jase McClellan out of the end zone, the Wolverines were behind again, 17-13, with 14:30 left in the fourth quarter.

Before Roman Wilson trotted the last few strides, quarterback J.J. McCarthy knew the Wolverines were about to tie the Crimson Tide late in regulation. Wilson jumped as he crossed the goal line with the perfect little four-yard swing pass. JUNFU HAN/ DETROIT FREE PRESS

Christian one year ago.

That loss in the semifinal round solidified the perception that Michigan couldn't beat the best teams outside of its conference footprint, that its rugged formula would lose its potency beyond the Big Ten. But it only made the Wolverines more determined to prove their skeptics wrong. Back in February, tailback Blake Corum proclaimed that the next Michigan team would win it all and go down in history. The goal was not only to return to this point but also get past it.

Now, under the fading sunlight, it all seemed to be slipping away and a brilliant performance, marked by a relentless defensive effort that featured six sacks of the elusive Jalen Milroe, was about to be rendered meaningless. But then something unexpected happened; Michigan dug deep, finding one more lifeline to extend its season and preserve its year-long fantasy.

"We never flinched," linebacker Michael Barrett said.

A team that weathered two separate suspensions of coach Jim Harbaugh, one controversy after another, a much-publicized cheating scandal and a season-ending injury to its best offensive lineman, reversed the tide in the game and its legacy.

"We promised our fans we were going to go win it all," Corum said. "We had to stand on that and we were able to come together. ... There was a lot that went into it."

Trailing by seven points with 4:41 left, the Wolverines embarked on an eight-play, 75-yard drive that revealed the grit of this team. Not surprisingly, it was spearheaded by Corum, the heartbeat of the team; McCarthy, its fearless leader; and Roman Wilson, the underdog receiver.

They delivered the biggest plays that launched the comeback. "The mentality that we

had going into that last drive, it was unbelievable," Wilson recalled.

On fourth-and-two at the Wolverines' 33, in what amounted to a do-or-die moment, McCarthy found Corum with a short pass that went for 27 yards, sustaining U-M's last-ditch effort and supplying it with momentum. The audacious quarterback then pushed the Wolverines into Alabama territory with a 16-yard run. The best was still to come, as Wilson made an acrobatic 29-yard catch on a tipped pass to carry Michigan to the edge of the Tide's end zone. Then he crossed the goal line two plays later on a four-yard reception that tied the score at 20 with 94 seconds left.

The dreams were still alive and faith had been restored among U-M fans.

What came next for them was sheer ecstasy.

In overtime, Corum slipped

through a hole, found a lane and then spun through a pack of defenders before arriving in the end zone. The 17-yard score sent the west side of the Rose Bowl into delirium.

But the biggest roars from the maize-and-blue faithful would come minutes later, when the Wolverines stopped Milroe two yards short of the end zone on fourth down — killing off Alabama's last chance and kicking off a wild celebration. The entire Michigan team emptied onto the field from the sideline, tossing helmets and throwing arms in the air. The fans behind the team jumped up and down.

Under the bright stadium lights, in the backdrop of Hollywood, everything was clear again now that Michigan was going to the national championship game.

It was an incredible sight. Michigan 27, Alabama 20.

"It doesn't get better than this," Corum said.

THE CHAMPS 113

Thousands upon thousands of Michiganders traveled west to have their voices heard. Besides a W, they were rewarded with sunny, 64-degree weather.
JUNFU HAN/ DETROIT FREE PRESS

THE PREAMBLE

▶▶▶ Known for decades for his shrewd moves, Nick Saban made a December hire that raised eyebrows in Ann Arbor. He plucked former Michigan linebackers coach George Helow from the ranks of the unemployed to be his special assistant. In February 2023, late in the coaching carousel, Jim Harbaugh had pushed aside Helow after two seasons to bring back Chris Partridge. Saban said that whenever the Crimson Tide made the playoffs he made a December hire because his staff had to spend two weeks on the road recruiting. He said he looked for someone to "give us a good scouting report about what we need to know." Helow previously served as a defensive intern for Saban in 2012, in the weight room during the spring and working with defensive coordinator Kirby Smart in the fall.

▶▶▶ Helow's defensive coordinator at U-M, Jesse Minter, didn't "put a lot of stock" into the potential impact of his former colleague on the Rose Bowl. "Props to him," Minter said. "He got

KIRBY LEE/USA TODAY SPORTS

Greeted by a lovely floral arrangement and an even lovelier trophy, Nick Saban and Jim Harbaugh shook hands and came out speaking at their joint news conference in Los Angeles.

hired by somebody." But linebacker Michael Barrett, whose career Helow helped resurrect, called Helow "just another obstacle in the way for us."

▶▶▶ Saban wouldn't provide bulletin board material by saying so out loud, but he had a decades-long disdain for Michigan from coaching in its shadow for a decade. He spent 1983-87 at Michigan State as defensive coordinator/secondary coach for George Perles and 1995-99 as the Spartans' head coach. Against U-M, Saban was 2-3 as an MSU assistant, including a 19-7 upset of the 13th-ranked Wolverines in 1984, a game in which Jim Harbaugh, in his first season as U-M's starting quarterback, suffered a broken arm. Saban also went 2-3 as MSU's head coach.

▶▶▶ At Alabama, Saban

twice delivered devastating blows to the Michigan program. In 2012's opener, at Cowboys Stadium, with coach Brady Hoke coming off an 11-2 debut season, the Tide steamrolled U-M, 41-14. On Jan. 1, 2020, Saban demanded a statement game from his team because of a two-loss season. Harbaugh's squad paid the price in a 35-16 loss in the Citrus Bowl. That victory served as a springboard for Saban's most recent national title in 2020, led by its three-headed monster of Mac Jones, Najee Harris and DeVonta Smith.

▶▶▶ The Crimson Tide boasted far more top-notch recruits than U-M in 2023. On the stat sheet, U-M held a significant edge in the defensive rankings. The offenses were similarly middle of the pack. U-M ranked No. 1 in scoring defense (9.5 points) and total defense (239.7 yards), No. 2 against the pass (152.6) and No. 6 against the run (87.1). In those categories, Alabama was 14th (tied), 16th, 27th and 31st. The Wolverines were favored by 1½ points.

And, just like that, it was over. Three hours and 32 minutes of drama ended when Michigan stopped Jalen Milroe two yards shy of the end zone. As the pile untangled, Derrick Moore (No. 8), credited with the tackle, had a hand on Milroe's helmet.
ROBERT HANASHIRO/USA TODAY SPORTS

THE STAND

▶▶▶ On Alabama's final play, Michigan knew what to expect. And it had nothing to do with stealing anybody's signs.

▶▶▶ "We knew they were going to get the ball in the playmaker's hands," linebacker Michael Barrett said of quarterback Jalen Milroe. "He's their best player; we knew he was going to get the ball in some way. We weren't going to sit back and be reactive; we were going to take it to him."

▶▶▶ After Blake Corum scored a touchdown and James Turner kicked the PAT on the first possession of overtime, Alabama needed to cover 25 yards to keep its season alive. On second-and-nine, Milroe dashed 15 yards for a

first-and-goal from the U-M 9. Then the defense went on the attack.

▶▶▶ On first down, Junior Colson stuffed Jase McClellan for no gain. On second down, Mason Graham exploded through the line and dumped McClellan for a five-yard loss. On third down, Milroe stood his ground against a furious rush and hit Jermaine Burton near the sideline inside the U-M 5. Josh Wallace, a transfer from UMass, made certain Burton couldn't bulldoze his way into the end zone.

▶▶▶ On fourth-and-goal from the U-M 3 ... Alabama called time ... and Michigan called time ... and Alabama called time again. Suddenly, a basketball game had broken out

at the Rose Bowl.

▶▶▶ The ball was on the right hash mark. Saban later said offensive coordinator Tommy Rees selected a play that the Tide practiced in case it needed a two-point conversion. Milroe was in the shotgun, eight yards from the goal line. The Wolverines loaded eight defenders into the box. Two Tide receivers were on the left side and one on the right side. Running back Roydell Williams stood a few yards off and behind Milroe's right shoulder and went in motion to his left.

▶▶▶ A low snap — poor snaps were a Bama bugaboo all game — got the play off to a sloppy start. Milroe caught the ball with both hands near his right foot and then

charged along the hash mark into the middle of the line. Derrick Moore, a sophomore edge rusher from Baltimore, received credit for the tackle, lowering his shoulders in a scrum right as Milroe lowered his. After they collided, a nanosecond later, Josaiah Stewart, a transfer from Coastal Carolina, drilled Milroe from the side. Down he went, two yards shy of the goal line.

▶▶▶ "We called a man coverage blitz," Barrett said. "Just like we thought, he tried to take it himself, and we shut it down."

▶▶▶ Saban said: "We didn't get it blocked, so it didn't work. We didn't execute it very well."

THE PLAY-BY-PLAY

▶▶▶ Michigan survived three uncharacteristic special teams mistakes. Semaj Morgan muffed a first-quarter punt that led to the game's first touchdown. Long snapper William Wagner fired a worm-burner that holder Tommy Doman couldn't corral on the point-after attempt when U-M took a 13-7 lead. Jake Thaw muffed a punt inside the U-M 5 in the final minute of regulation but gathered the ball inches from the goal line.

▶▶▶ On the game's first play, J.J. McCarthy failed to throw away a pass to the sideline, and Alabama's Caleb Downs intercepted it at the U-M 31. However, a video review showed Downs was out of bounds, ever so barely, as he jumped for the ball, making him ineligible to touch it. After that, McCarthy completed 17 of 26 passes for 221 yards and three touchdowns and rushed three times for 25 yards. He threw no picks, wasn't sacked and recovered an off-target pitch from Blake Corum.

▶▶▶ Michigan outgained Alabama, 351-288. The Wolverines' points came on an eight-yard reception by Corum, a 38-yard catch-and-run by Tyler Morris, a four-yard reception by Roman Wilson and a 17-yard OT run by Corum.

▶▶▶ The MVPs were McCarthy on offense and tackle Mason Graham on defense. A 6-foot-3, 318-pound disruptor on the line all day, Graham made four tackles, including one for a five-yard loss in overtime.

THE PRIME NUMBER

44

Yards Michigan gained in the second half before embarking on a 75-yard drive to tie Alabama late in the final quarter.

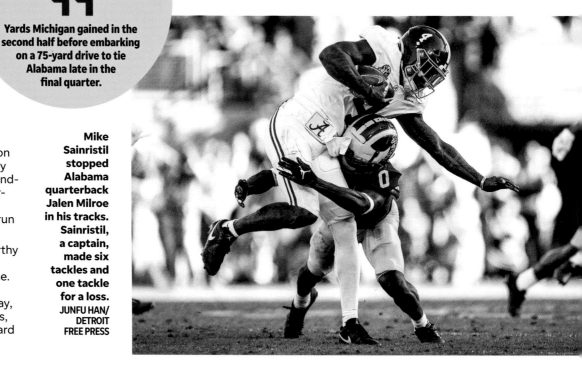

Asked where the game ranked, J.J. McCarthy, the offensive MVP, replied: "The greatest of all time. ... We got one more, though. We got one more."
JUNFU HAN/ DETROIT FREE PRESS

Mike Sainristil stopped Alabama quarterback Jalen Milroe in his tracks. Sainristil, a captain, made six tackles and one tackle for a loss.
JUNFU HAN/ DETROIT FREE PRESS

Jim Harbaugh hoisted the trophy as confetti descended on a makeshift stage at the Rose Bowl. "It's a togetherness," he said. "We were going to overcome anything that was inside this stadium." JUNFU HAN/DETROIT FREE PRESS

THE PROCLAMATIONS

▶▶▶ **COACH JIM HARBAUGH:** "It's almost been an unfair advantage, all the things that the team has gone through. We don't care anymore. Don't care what people say. Don't care about anything that comes up. We just know we're going to overcome it because it's unanimous support from every single guy on the team."

▶▶▶ **LINEBACKER MICHAEL BARRETT:** "They really haven't seen a defense like ours. They weren't prepared for the movements and the schemes that we have."

▶▶▶ **ALABAMA COACH NICK SABAN:** "We just didn't finish the last four minutes of the game like we would like to, and we're all very disappointed."

▶▶▶ **OFFENSIVE LINEMAN LADARIUS HENDERSON:** "Everyone in the stadium thought a quarterback run was coming. If I were them, I probably would have done the exact same thing."

JUNFU HAN/DETROIT FREE PRESS

Coach Jim Harbaugh and defensive lineman Josaiah Stewart, a transfer from Coastal Carolina, basked in the glory of victory.

THE PRESS BOX

▶▶▶ **PAUL MYERBERG, USA TODAY:** "The second overtime game in playoff semifinal history ended with a puzzling call: Alabama running quarterback Jalen Milroe right into the teeth of the Michigan defense on fourth-and-goal. That stop tells the story of the entire year for the Wolverines, who have simply been the more physical and aggressive opponent in marquee wins against Penn State, Ohio State and the Tide."

▶▶▶ **SHAWN WINDSOR, DETROIT FREE PRESS:** "Unfair advantage? Probably not. Yet these Wolverines turned adversity into fuel like no other team Harbaugh has had in Ann Arbor, precisely because he — and they — care about what they've been hearing."

THE POSTSCRIPT

▶▶▶ From the Where Are They Now Dept.:

▶▶▶ Former analyst Connor Stalions attended the Rose Bowl in pretty decent seats. An Instagram post from former U-M defensive end Chase Winovich, who retired in the fall after five years in the NFL, showed Stalions wearing a blue Michigan hoodie with a necklace made of roses. Chris Branch of The Athletic offered a great line: "The guy loves buying tickets to watch Michigan opponents."

▶▶▶ Tom Brady, QB2 on Michigan's 1997 championship team, posted pictures of himself on Instagram wearing Michigan vs. Everybody bracelets. Then he posted a celebration video in which he recorded his TV screen, panned to himself — shirtless — and turned his device back to the screen.

Everything old is new again, like the Wolverines as champs — and doing it with a dominant ground game.

JUNFU HAN/DETROIT FREE PRESS

Senior tailback Blake Corum proved elusive as ever in his final game as a Wolverine. He rushed 21 times for 134 yards (6.4 a carry) and two touchdowns.

A run for the ages

By Tony Garcia
THE BIG PICTURE

Michigan's football season — full of tumult and chaos, scandal and smears — ended with confetti falling, tears streaming and one resounding message: *We told you so.*

The first two times junior tailback Donovan Edwards touched the football he ran for long touchdowns.
MELANIE MAXWELL/DETROIT FREE PRESS

Jack Harbaugh, a U-M assistant coach back in the day, hugged his son Jim, now a title-winning U-M coach. JUNFU HAN/DFP

The Wolverines ran over Washington early, then late, 34-13, in the College Football Playoff title game at NRG Stadium in Houston and won the 2023 national championship in Jim Harbaugh's ninth season in Ann Arbor.

It was the program's first national title since it went 12-0 in 1997 and marked just the fourth time in NCAA history an FBS champion had gone 15-0 (Clemson, 2018; LSU, 2019; Georgia, 2022).

"It couldn't have gone better," Harbaugh said afterward. "It went exactly how we wanted it to go to win every game. The off-the-field issues, we're innocent and we stood strong and tall because we knew we were innocent. And I'd like to point that out."

Harbaugh said it felt good to no longer be the only coach in the family without a national championship. His father won a Division I-AA title with Western Kentucky and brother John won a Super Bowl with the Baltimore Ravens by beating Jim's San Francisco 49ers 11 years ago.

"I can now sit at the big person's table in the family," Harbaugh said.

Blake Corum ran for 134 yards and two fourth-quarter touchdowns as the top-ranked Wolverines — undeterred by suspensions and a sign-stealing case that shadowed the program — completed a three-year surge after losing in the playoff semifinals the past two seasons.

The Wolverines, whose ground game didn't quite match its results the past two years, put it all together when it mattered most. They ran 38 times for 303 yards and four scores, which included three rushes of more than 40 yards in the first quarter.

Michigan's defense also was an important story in the game. The Wolverines held Michael Penix Jr. and the Huskies' prolific passing game to one touchdown while intercepting the Heisman Trophy runner-up twice.

Washington entered play with the No. 1 passing attack (350 yards a game) and a top-10 scoring offense (37.6 points a game), but the Huskies hadn't seen a defense such as U-M's, which ranked No. 1 in scoring and No. 2 against the pass.

Penix's remarkable six-year college career ended with maybe his worst performance of the season. Usually unfazed by pressure, Penix was not nearly as precise against a Michigan defense that took away his signature deep throws.

Penix completed only 27 of 51 passes for 255 yards, and the Wolverines held the Huskies to 20 rushes for 46 yards (2.3 yards an attempt) and two of 14 third-down conversions.

"That was a spectacular game by our defense," Harbaugh said.

Defensive coordinator Jesse Minter thought his unit was overlooked heading into the game.

"Honestly, it was another week of hearing all about the other team's offense, and how good they were," Minter said.

His voice carried no anger, but you could sense the chip on his shoulder.

"You know what, nobody really talks about how good our defense was, and so we took that personal," Minter said. "The players took it personal. You know, we were at media day, and all we got asked about was how good their quarterback was, how good their receivers were, how good the O-line was. And we answered the bell."

The Wolverines sealed their title when Corum, who scored the winning touchdown in overtime against Alabama in the Rose Bowl, blasted in from the 1-yard line with 3:37 left to put Michigan up by 21 and set off another rousing rendition of The Victors from the band.

Fellow running back Donovan Edwards gave the Wolverines an early 14-3 lead when he scored twice in the first quarter. The West Bloomfield alumnus took his first touch of the night 41 yards to the house, which was announced as the second-longest touchdown run in CFP title game history.

That record stood for less than eight minutes after he ripped off a 46-yard burst to the right side.

Edwards finished with six runs for 104 yards and two scores; he and Corum became the first teammates to run for more than 100 yards in a CFP title game.

Quarterback J.J. McCarthy wasn't as crisp as he was in the Rose Bowl, but he made just enough plays. After a tough stretch in the middle of the game in which he completed just two of 10 passes,

At the Rose Bowl, Jim Harbaugh scrambled along the sideline to avoid a Gatorade bath from his players. And then he tried to do so again at Houston. He escaped once, but while he was waiting for a TV interview, his Wolverines finally drenched him.

McCarthy hit three in a row in the second half, then later when backed up made scrambles of 22 yards and 12 yards. Those didn't lead to points, but they did flip the field and eat up clock.

He finished with 10 of 18 passing for 140 yards.

U-M almost looked as if it would hold Washington without a touchdown in the first half, but the Huskies put together an 11-play, 61-yard drive to score with 42 seconds left and trailed 17-10 at halftime.

Will Johnson came up with an interception to start the second half and from there the Huskies never got much going. After both teams made a field goal for a 20-13 score, Corum, U-M's modern touchdown record-holder, broke a tackle and trucked his way in from 12 yards out, and Michigan went up, 27-13, with 7:09 to play in the game.

Washington reached Michigan territory one last time when Penix hit Rome Odunze on a 44-yard bomb to the 27. But on fourth-and-13 from the 30, Mike Sainristil came away with an 81-yard interception return, his sixth of the season.

"When a play needs to be made, Mike Sainristil has made it," Harbaugh said. "When a play needs to be made, Blake Corum makes it. When a play needs to be made, Will Johnson makes it. When a play needs to be made, J.J. McCarthy makes it.

"We've just got great players. We've got great players that unanimously support each other."

Corum was named the game's most valuable offensive player and Will Johnson the defensive MVP.

"I'll leave y'all with this," Corum said while standing on a stage as maize-and-blue confetti fluttered in the air around him. "Business is finished."

Michigan fans came out in droves to Houston to cheer their team to its first national championship in 26 years. The Wolverines lay claim to 12 such titles, including four in the modern age.

THE PREAMBLE

▶▶▶ For the first time in 26 years, the Wolverines were one victory from a national championship. And just as in the 1997 season, their final test hailed from the Evergreen State. On Jan. 1, 1998, Michigan beat Washington State, 21-16, at the Rose Bowl and ended up sharing the title with Nebraska. This time, at NRG Stadium in Houston, sharing wasn't possible. Michigan or Washington — each 14-0 — would win the last four-team College Football Playoff. The field would be expanded to 12 teams for the 2024 season. The Wolverines were installed as 4½-point favorites.

▶▶▶ Washington had lived the entire season on a razor's edge. Their last 10 victories were by 10 points or fewer. Their past five were one-possession outcomes. Every coach and fan knew that wasn't sustainable — unless a team truly was one of destiny. And the Huskies believed.

▶▶▶ They boasted a potent offense led by Michael Penix Jr., a transfer from Indiana who finished second in the Heisman Trophy voting. He threw to a group of skilled receivers, led by Rome Odunze, a finalist for the Biletnikoff Award. Even though the Huskies didn't run the ball a lot, Dillon Johnson rushed for nearly 1,200 yards, but he suffered a knee injury against Texas in the semifinals. Still, he was expected to play. The Huskies owned the country's top passing offense (350.0 yards a game) and ninth-best scoring offense (37.6 points).

▶▶▶ On defense, well, the Huskies tried not to play defense as much as possible. They were ranked 88th in total defense (404.1 yards), 121st against the pass (267.1) and 41st against the run (137.1). To most pundits, the keys to the game were whether the Huskies could stop Michigan's ground game and whether the Wolverines could pressure Penix, known to be a bit erratic without a clean pocket. The Wolverines were ranked No. 1 in scoring defense (10.2 points) and total defense (243.1 yards) and No. 2 in passing defense (150.0).

▶▶▶ The resume of Washington coach Kalen DeBoer included a Washtenaw County tie and a believe-it-or-not winning percentage. He spent three seasons at Eastern Michigan (2014-16) as Chris Creighton's offensive coordinator. Before that, he won three NAIA championships and 67 of 70 games with Sioux Falls. At Fresno State, he went 12-6. At Washington, he was 25-2. As a college coach, DeBoer, only 49, was 104-11 — a .904 winning percentage.

Defensive lineman Kenneth Grant, a 339-pound sophomore, leveled Michael Penix Jr. for a 12-yard sack in the second quarter.

After his sack, Kenneth Grant celebrated by letting out a primal yell.

THE PLAY-BY-PLAY

▶▶▶ With less than five minutes gone in the game, Michigan backup running back Donovan Edwards blew through an opening and ran 41 yards for a touchdown for a 7-3 lead. Later in the quarter, he went 46 yards for another TD. In U-M's previous 14 games, Edwards had scored three times and gained 393 yards.

▶▶▶ On the first play of the second half, U-M defensive back Will Johnson intercepted a Michael Penix Jr. pass at the Washington 32. Six plays later, a James Turner field goal gave the Wolverines a 20-10 lead. With less than five minutes left in the fourth quarter, the Huskies drove to the Michigan 30. On fourth-and-13, Mike Sainristil intercepted a pass and returned it 81 yards to the Washington 8. Blake Corum scored two plays later. Final: Michigan 34, Washington 13.

▶▶▶ Corum gained 134 yards in the game, and almost half came on one run. On the last play of the first quarter, Corum raced 59 yards to the Washington 20. Four plays later, a Turner field goal gave the Wolverines a 17-3 lead.

THE PROCLAMATIONS

▶▶▶ **OFFENSIVE LINEMAN ZAK ZINTER:** "This means everything. The reason we came back was winning a national championship, and we just did it."

▶▶▶ **U-M PRESIDENT SANTA ONO:** "Applications are up, donations are up, school pride is up, so it's incredible. It brings us together like almost nothing else."

▶▶▶ **ATHLETIC DIRECTOR WARDE MANUEL:** "It means my gut was right."

▶▶▶ **WIDE RECEIVER ROMAN WILSON:** "We played a lot of good teams. This year, we played a lot of guys who are gonna go to the league and do really good, and, you know, we just had this amazing season, a lot of clutch plays and made it to the natty. It's unreal."

Despite a broken leg, Zak Zinter took his turn hoisting the trophy.
JUNFU HAN/DFP

THE PRESS BOX

▶▶▶ **PAUL MYERBERG, USA TODAY:** "The at-long-last crowning of the Wolverines is the culmination of all the promise and potential that accompanied Harbaugh's return eight years ago. Through it all — the struggles to get over the hump against Ohio State, the disastrous COVID season, the recruiting violations, the sign-stealing scandal — Harbaugh never lost sight of the program he wanted to build: one that stayed the course, eschewed beauty points and embraced his throwback style."

▶▶▶ **SHAWN WINDSOR, DETROIT FREE PRESS:** "He won the way he has always won, everywhere he has been, and no matter how much football changes, Jim Harbaugh always believed in the kind of football his team just played to win the national championship. It just took him awhile to show it at Michigan, show that defense and a ground game are as lethal a combo as ever, and when a team has the best defense and a bulldozing ground game? There is no rung of football that can't be conquered."

▶▶▶ **MAX OLSON, THE ATHLETIC:** "Jim Harbaugh's way worked. In a sport dominated by SEC superpowers for nearly two decades, Michigan figured out how to beat the house."

MELANIE MAXWELL/DETROIT FREE PRESS

When a Wolverine scored, quarterback J.J. McCarthy pretended to place a crown on his head. McCarthy did so twice for Donovan Edwards in the first quarter.

A perfect night for J.J. McCarthy! On the field, he directed his Wolverines to their first national championship since 1997. He threw for 140 yards and ran for 31. He was on stage for the trophy presentation. Along the way, he shared a kiss with his girlfriend.

Cornerback Will Johnson sported a championship belt during the postgame festivities.

THE PRIME NUMBER

3

Combined third-down conversions by the Wolverines and the Huskies. Michigan went 1-for-10 on third down; Washington went 2-for-14.

THE POSTSCRIPT

▶▶▶ How ESPN and Michigan's radio network called the final seconds:

▶▶▶ **CHRIS FOWLER ON TELEVISION:** "There are people out there that believe that whatever Michigan does is tainted. That's up to you to decide. But ... hail, hail, Michigan! They are the champions of college football 2023." As the final seconds ticked off, the band struck up The Victors and the celebration started, Fowler and partner Kirk Herbstreit stayed silent for 32 seconds.

▶▶▶ **DOUG KARSCH ON RADIO:** "The Wolverines have won a national championship! Wolverine players, Wolverine alums, Michigan fans everywhere, Jim Harbaugh and your staff, your team is the No. 1 team in America as the clock ticks down and Michigan completes a 15-0, national championship season here in Houston. Bedlam!"

THE CHAMPS 125

HONOR ROLL

Meet the best of the best when accolades were handed out.

OL RAHEEM ANDERSON
DETROIT
▶▶▶ Michigan scout team offensive player of the year

DB NICO ANDRIGHETTO
MOUNTAIN VIEW, CALIF.
▶▶▶ Michigan scout team special teams player of the year

TE AJ BARNER
AURORA, OHIO
▶▶▶ Coaches All-Big Ten honorable mention

OT KARSEN BARNHART
PAW PAW
▶▶▶ Coaches All-Big Ten second team
▶▶▶ Media All-Big Ten third team

LB MICHAEL BARRETT
VALDOSTA, GA.
▶▶▶ Coaches All-Big Ten third team
▶▶▶ Media All-Big Ten honorable mention
▶▶▶ Michigan best linebacker award

TE MAX BREDESON
HARTLAND, WIS.
▶▶▶ Michigan offensive most improved player

LB JUNIOR COLSON
BRENTWOOD, TENN.
▶▶▶ Lott IMPACT Trophy (on, off field)
▶▶▶ Coaches and media All-Big Ten second team
▶▶▶ Michigan co-defensive player of the year
▶▶▶ Michigan Toughest Player award

RB BLAKE CORUM
MARSHALL, VA.
▶▶▶ All-America first team (AFCA)
▶▶▶ All-America second team (FWAA, Walter Camp)
▶▶▶ All-America third team (AP)
▶▶▶ Big Ten running back of the year
▶▶▶ Coaches and Media All-Big Ten first team
▶▶▶ National comeback player of the year
▶▶▶ National championship offensive player of the game
▶▶▶ AFCA Good Works team captain

▶▶▶ Michigan offensive player of the year
▶▶▶ Michigan Blue Collar award

P TOMMY DOMAN
WEST BLOOMFIELD
▶▶▶ Coaches All-Big Ten third team
▶▶▶ Media All-Big Ten honorable mention
▶▶▶ Michigan most improved special teams player

DL MASON GRAHAM
ANAHEIM, CALIF.
▶▶▶ All-America second team (Sporting News)
▶▶▶ Coaches All-Big Ten first team
▶▶▶ Media All-Big Ten third team
▶▶▶ Michigan Woodley-Graham award (top defensive lineman or outside linebacker)
▶▶▶ Rose Bowl defensive MVP

DL KENNETH GRANT
MERRILLVILLE, IND.
▶▶▶ Coaches All-Big Ten second team
▶▶▶ Media All-Big Ten third team
▶▶▶ Michigan Woodley-Graham award (top defensive lineman or outside linebacker)
▶▶▶ Michigan most improved defensive player

DL JAYLEN HARRELL
TAMPA, FLA.
▶▶▶ Coaches and media All-Big Ten honorable mention

OT LADARIUS HENDERSON
WAXAHACHIE, TEXAS
▶▶▶ Coaches All-Big Ten first team
▶▶▶ Media All-Big Ten second team

DL KRIS JENKINS
OLNEY, MD.
▶▶▶ All-America second team (AFCA, FWAA)
▶▶▶ All-America third team (AP)
▶▶▶ Coaches and media All-Big Ten second team
▶▶▶ Michigan co-defensive player of the year
▶▶▶ Michigan Ufer award (enthusiasm)

WR CORNELIUS JOHNSON
GREENWICH, CONN.
▶▶▶ Media All-Big Ten honorable

mention

DB WILL JOHNSON
DETROIT
▶▶▶ Coaches and media All-Big Ten first team
▶▶▶ National championship defensive player of the game

OG TREVOR KEEGAN
CRYSTAL LAKE, ILL.
▶▶▶ Coaches and media All-Big Ten second team

DB CADEN KOLESAR
WESTLAKE, OHIO
▶▶▶ Michigan special teams player of the year

TE COLSTON LOVELAND
GOODING, IDAHO
▶▶▶ Coaches All-Big Ten first team
▶▶▶ Media All-Big Ten second team
▶▶▶ Michigan co-offensive skill player of the year

QB J.J. MCCARTHY
LA GRANGE PARK, ILL.
▶▶▶ Big Ten quarterback of the year
▶▶▶ Coaches and media All-Big Ten first team
▶▶▶ Michigan most valuable player
▶▶▶ Rose Bowl offensive MVP

DL BRAIDEN MCGREGOR
PORT HURON
▶▶▶ Coaches and media All-Big Ten honorable mention

DL DERRICK MOORE
BALTIMORE
▶▶▶ Coaches and media All-Big Ten honorable mention

LB HAYDEN MOORE
PARKER, COLO.
▶▶▶ Michigan scout team defensive player of the year

DB ROD MOORE
CLAYTON, OHIO
▶▶▶ Coaches All-Big Ten third team
▶▶▶ Media All-Big Ten honorable mention

WR/KR SEMAJ MORGAN
WEST BLOOMFIELD

▶▶▶ Coaches and media All-Big Ten honorable mention
▶▶▶ Michigan rookie of the year

C DRAKE NUGENT
LONE TREE, COLO.
▶▶▶ Coaches and media All-Big Ten first team

DB MAKARI PAIGE
WEST BLOOMFIELD
▶▶▶ Coaches All-Big Ten honorable mention

DB MIKE SAINRISTIL
EVERETT, MASS.
▶▶▶ All-America first team (Sporting News)
▶▶▶ Media All-Big Ten first team
▶▶▶ Coaches All-Big Ten second team
▶▶▶ Michigan co-defensive player of the year
▶▶▶ Michigan defensive skill player of the year

DL JOSAIAH STEWART
BRONX, N.Y.
▶▶▶ Coaches All-Big Ten honorable mention

K JAMES TURNER
SALINE
▶▶▶ Coaches All-Big Ten second team
▶▶▶ Media All-Big Ten honorable mention
▶▶▶ Michigan specialist of the year

DB JOSH WALLACE
BOWIE, MD.
▶▶▶ Coaches and media All-Big Ten honorable mention

WR ROMAN WILSON
MAUI, HAWAII
▶▶▶ Coaches and media All-Big Ten second team
▶▶▶ Michigan co-offensive skill player of the year

OL ZAK ZINTER
NORTH ANDOVER, MASS.
▶▶▶ All-America first team (consensus, AP, AFCA, FWAA, Sporting News, Walter Camp)
▶▶▶ Coaches and media All-Big Ten first team
▶▶▶ Michigan top offensive lineman award
▶▶▶ Michigan scholarship award

TEAM 144

NO	NAME	POS	HT	WT	CL	HOMETOWN
0	Darrius Clemons	WR	6-3	212	So.	Portland, Ore.
0	Mike Sainristil	DB	5-10	182	Gr.	Everett, Mass.
1	Amorion Walker	DB	6-3	180	So.	Ponchatoula, La.
1	Roman Wilson	WR	6-0	192	Sr.	Maui, Hawaii
2	Blake Corum	RB	5-8	213	Sr.	Marshall, Va.
2	Will Johnson	DB	6-2	202	So.	Detroit
3	Fredrick Moore	WR	6-1	180	Fr.	St. Louis
3	Keon Sabb	DB	6-1	208	So.	Glassboro, N.J.
4	Jayden Denegal	QB	6-5	235	So.	Apple Valley, Calif.
4	Micah Pollard	LB	6-2	221	So.	Jacksonville, Fla.
5	Karmello English	WR	5-11	190	Fr.	Phenix City, Ala.
5	Josaiah Stewart	EDGE	6-1	245	Jr.	Bronx, N.Y.
6	Brandyn Hillman	DB	6-0	200	Fr.	Portsmouth, Va.
6	Cornelius Johnson	WR	6-3	208	Gr.	Greenwich, Conn.
7	Donovan Edwards	RB	6-1	210	Jr.	West Bloomfield
7	Makari Paige	DB	6-4	208	Sr.	West Bloomfield
8	Derrick Moore	EDGE	6-3	258	So.	Baltimore
8	Tyler Morris	WR	5-11	185	So.	Bolingbrook, Ill.
9	J.J. McCarthy	QB	6-3	202	Jr.	La Grange Park, Ill.
9	Rod Moore	DB	6-0	198	Jr.	Clayton, Ohio
10	Zeke Berry	DB	5-11	192	So.	Pittsburg, Calif.
10	Alex Orji	QB	6-3	236	So.	Sachse, Texas
12	Kendrick Bell	WR	6-2	180	Fr.	Kansas City, Mo.
12	Josh Wallace	DB	6-0	190	Gr.	Bowie, Md.
13	Jack Tuttle	QB	6-4	210	Gr.	San Marcos, Calif.
13	DJ Waller Jr.	DB	6-3	205	Fr.	Youngstown, Ohio
14	Jack Grusser	WR	6-0	175	Fr.	Franklin Lakes, N.J.
14	Kody Jones	DB	5-11	195	So.	Memphis, Tenn.
15	Ernest Hausmann	LB	6-2	237	So.	Columbus, Neb.
16	Semaj Bridgeman	LB	6-2	246	Fr.	Philadelphia
16	Davis Warren	QB	6-2	195	Jr.	Los Angeles
17	Marlin Klein	TE	6-6	250	So.	Cologne, Germany
17	Braiden McGregor	EDGE	6-6	267	Sr.	Port Huron
18	Colston Loveland	TE	6-5	245	So.	Gooding, Idaho
18	Ja'Den McBurrows	DB	5-11	200	Jr.	Fort Lauderdale, Fla.
19	Tommy Doman	K/P	6-4	215	Jr.	West Bloomfield
19	Jason Hewlett	LB	6-2	224	Fr.	Youngstown, Ohio
20	Jyaire Hill	DB	6-2	181	Fr.	Kankakee, Ill.
20	Kalel Mullings	RB	6-2	239	Sr.	West Roxbury, Mass.
22	Tavierre Dunlap	RB	6-0	229	Jr.	Del Valle, Texas
23	Michael Barrett	LB	6-0	239	Gr.	Valdosta, Ga.
23	CJ Stokes	RB	5-10	205	So.	Columbia, S.C.
24	Cole Cabana	RB	6-0	198	Fr.	Dexter
24	Myles Pollard	DB	6-1	190	So.	Brentwood, Tenn.
25	Junior Colson	LB	6-3	247	Jr.	Brentwood, Tenn.
26	Rayshaun Benny	DL	6-4	296	Jr.	Detroit
26	Jake Thaw	WR	6-1	192	So.	Westport, Conn.
27	Christian Bartholomew	WR	6-0	187	Sr.	Galesburg
27	Tyler McLaurin	EDGE	6-3	247	Jr.	Bolingbrook, Ill.
28	Benjamin Hall	RB	5-11	234	Fr.	Acworth, Ga.
28	Quinten Johnson	DB	5-11	200	Gr.	Silver Spring, Md.
29	Joshua Nichols	DB	5-10	196	So.	Detroit
29	Joey Velazquez	LB	6-0	222	Gr.	Columbus, Ohio
30	Will Rolapp	WR	6-0	198	Sr.	Darien, Conn.
30	Jimmy Rolder	LB	6-2	233	So.	Orland Park, Ill.
31	Nico Andrighetto	DB	5-9	190	So.	Mountain View, Calif.
31	Leon Franklin	RB	5-9	208	Gr.	Southfield
32	Jaylen Harrell	EDGE	6-4	242	Sr.	Tampa, Fla.
32	James Turner	K	6-0	196	Gr.	Saline
33	German Green	DB	6-2	190	So.	DeSoto, Texas
34	Jaydon Hood	LB	6-1	225	Jr.	Fort Lauderdale, Fla.
35	Logan Forbes	WR	6-2	193	So.	Clarkston
35	Caden Kolesar	DB	5-10	195	Gr.	Westlake, Ohio
36	Keshaun Harris	DB	5-11	192	So.	Lansing
37	Micah Davis	DB	6-1	199	Fr.	Dexter
37	Danny Hughes	RB	6-0	208	Gr.	Naperville, Ill.
38	Grayson Dee	LB	6-1	228	Fr.	Pittsburgh
38	Bryce Wilcox	DB	5-11	188	So.	Sharpsburg, Ga.
39	Jack MacKinnon	LB	6-4	244	Fr.	Sarasota, Fla.
39	Joe Taylor	WR	5-10	191	Jr.	Chelsea
40	Josh Beetham	TE	6-5	242	Sr.	Yorkville, Ill.
40	Christian Boivin	LB	6-0	220	Jr.	Traverse City
41	Bryson Kuzdzal	RB	5-11	193	Fr.	Ada
41	Joshua Luther	DB	5-9	182	Gr.	Clarkston
42	TJ Guy	EDGE	6-4	250	Jr.	Mansfield, Mass.
42	Jalen Hoffman	TE	6-3	225	Fr.	Lake Braddock, Va.
43	Jesse Madden	DB	6-1	180	Jr.	Oakland, Calif.
43	Deakon Tonielli	TE	6-5	251	Fr.	Oswego, Ill.
44	Max Bredeson	TE	6-2	240	Jr.	Hartland, Wis.
44	Hayden Moore	LB	6-2	226	Fr.	Parker, Colo.
45	Noah Howes	TE	6-4	242	Jr.	Rochester
45	Greg Tarr	LS	6-2	205	Sr.	Washington, Mich.
46	Cameron Calhoun	DB	6-0	173	Fr.	Cincinnati
46	Brandon Mann	TE	6-3	231	So.	Franklin
49	Henry Donohue	RB	5-11	209	Jr.	Bronxville, N.Y.
49	William Wagner	LS	6-2	255	Gr.	Alpharetta, Ga.
50	Amir Herring	OL	6-3	300	Fr.	Southfield
50	Jerome Nichols	LB	6-0	235	Sr.	Belleville
51	Brooks Bahr	DL	6-5	298	Fr.	Lake Forest, Ill.
51	Greg Crippen	OL	6-4	309	Jr.	Northborough, Mass.
52	Karsen Barnhart	OL	6-5	316	Gr.	Paw Paw
52	Kechaun Bennett	EDGE	6-4	257	Jr.	Suffield, Conn.
53	Liam Groulx	LB	6-0	227	Fr.	Charlotte, N.C.
53	Trente Jones	OL	6-4	325	Gr.	Grayson, Ga.
54	Joel Metzger	LB	6-1	226	Jr.	Battle Creek
54	Cole Morgan	OL	6-4	270	Fr.	Princeton, N.J.
55	Nathan Efobi	OL	6-3	285	Fr.	Cumming, Ga.
55	Mason Graham	DL	6-3	318	So.	Anaheim, Calif.
56	Dominick Giudice	OL	6-4	305	Jr.	Freehold, N.J.
57	Trevor Andrews	LB	6-1	224	Jr.	Brentwood, Tenn.
58	Giovanni El-Hadi	OL	6-5	318	Jr.	Sterling Heights
58	Breeon Ishmail	EDGE	6-3	262	Fr.	Hamilton, Ohio
59	John Weidenbach	LB	6-0	215	Fr.	Naperville, Ill.
60	Drake Nugent	OL	6-2	301	Gr.	Lone Tree, Colo.
61	Noah Stewart	OL	6-7	292	Sr.	Muskegon
62	Raheem Anderson	OL	6-3	316	Jr.	Detroit
64	James Kavouklis	OL/LS	6-1	279	So.	Tampa, Fla.
65	Zak Zinter	OL	6-6	322	Sr.	North Andover, Mass.
70	Peter Simmons	DL	6-1	283	Jr.	Bonita Springs, Fla.
71	Evan Link	OL	6-6	307	Fr.	Burke, Va.
72	Tristan Bounds	OL	6-8	305	Jr.	Wallingford, Conn.
73	LaDarius Henderson	OL	6-4	315	Gr.	Waxahachie, Texas
74	Reece Atteberry	DL	6-5	309	Sr.	Aurora, Colo.
75	Andrew Gentry	OL	6-7	327	So.	Littleton, Colo.
76	Connor Jones	OL	6-6	320	So.	Monument, Colo.
77	Trevor Keegan	OL	6-6	320	Gr.	Crystal Lake, Ill.
78	Kenneth Grant	DL	6-3	339	So.	Merrillville, Ind.
78	Myles Hinton	OL	6-6	340	Sr.	John's Creek, Ga.
79	Jeffrey Persi	OL	6-8	320	Sr.	Mission Viejo, Calif.
80	Eamonn Dennis	WR	5-10	188	Sr.	Worcester, Mass.
81	Peyton O'Leary	WR	6-3	200	Jr.	Byfield, Mass.
82	Semaj Morgan	WR	5-10	176	Fr.	West Bloomfield
83	Zack Marshall	TE	6-4	232	Fr.	Carlsbad, Calif.
84	Dale Chesson	WR	6-0	190	Gr.	St. Louis
85	Cristian Dixon	WR	6-2	197	Jr.	Santa Ana, Calif.
86	Zach Peterson	WR	6-1	190	Gr.	Roswell, Ga.
88	Matthew Hibner	TE	6-5	254	Sr.	Burke, Va.
89	AJ Barner	TE	6-6	251	Sr.	Aurora, Ohio
89	Alessandro Lorenzetti	DL	6-5	301	So.	Montreal, Québec
90	Hudson Hollenbeck	K	6-2	208	So.	Collierville, Tenn.
90	Aymeric Koumba	EDGE	6-5	254	Fr.	Bordeaux, France
91	Evan Boutorwick	LS	6-3	230	So.	Macomb
91	Cameron Brandt	DL	6-4	277	Jr.	Chatsworth, Calif.
92	Stone Anderson	K/P	6-2	190	Fr.	Deerfield, Mass.
92	Ike Iwunnah	DL	6-3	313	Jr.	Garland, Texas
93	Joey Klunder	EDGE	6-3	276	So.	Grosse Pointe
94	Kris Jenkins	DL	6-3	305	Sr.	Olney, Md.
95	Trey Pierce	DL	6-2	300	Fr.	Chicago
96	Enow Etta	EDGE	6-5	295	Fr.	Keller, Texas
97	Chibi Anwunah	EDGE	6-5	268	So.	Canton
97	Cordell Jones-McNally	K/P	5-8	175	Fr.	Marcellus
99	Cam Goode	DL	6-1	314	Gr.	Washington, D.C.
99	Adam Samaha	K	5-11	185	Fr.	Ypsilanti

CL denotes years in college not eligibility status

For defensive back Mike Sainristil and offensive lineman Trevor Keegan, the season ended with a championship and a hug for the ages.
MELANIE MAXWELL/ DETROIT FREE PRESS